PRINCESS MARGARET

PRINCESS MARGARET

an informal biography

by GORDON LANGLEY HALL

illustrated with photographs

MACRAE SMITH COMPANY: PHILADELPHIA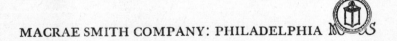

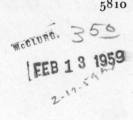

FOR BELLE DONNELLY HAYES

OF SANTA BARBARA, CALIFORNIA
who has always been kind to me.

Contents

contents continued

Biron

Our wooing doth not end
*   like an old play;*
Jack hath not Jill; these
*   ladies' courtesy*
Might well have made our sport
*   a comedy.*

King

Come, sir, it wants a
*   twelvemonth and a day,*
And then 'twill end.

Biron

*   That's too long*
for a play.

WILLIAM SHAKESPEARE:
Love's Labours Lost.
Act V. Scene II.

Author's Note

Princess Margaret has brought a touch of spring into many people's lives. She has become the very symbol of all a twentieth century princess should be.

While covering her royal tours in my capacity as a journalist, I have often been touched by the wonderful way she has with people. Watching a baby bathed in Africa, chatting with straw workers in a West Indian market place or playing a guitar for children in a Sussex orphanage—at all times Princess Margaret seems to sparkle. Like her mother, the "Dolly Princess," as the West Indians call her, has inherited the common touch.

There are still many people who are quite convinced that the Princess's life is one long round of night clubs and parties. Perhaps this book will help dispel such a mistaken impression.

In such a close family circle as Margaret's it is often difficult to isolate one member from the rest, so I have included special chapters dealing with close relatives who are or have been particularly dear to her.

My thanks are due to the following for helping to channel my research material: Isabelle Angus, Isabel L. Whitney, Marjorie Chambers Mitchell, Shirley Worth, Joseph A. Scaltro, and my mother, Marjorie Hall Copper.

GORDON LANGLEY HALL

Leon County Public Library

LCL2 Agency
01/21/1996
05:28 PM

YOU HAVE CHECKED OUT THE ITEMS LISTED
BELOW. THE DUE DATE FOR EACH ITEM IS
LISTED. PLEASE RETURN THE ITEMS ON OR
BEFORE THE DATE(S) LISTED. THANK YOU.
"PLEASE KEEP THIS RECEIPT"

Princess Margaret, an informal biography
31260001489155
Due: 02/11/1996

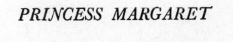

PRINCESS MARGARET

THE TERROR OF BUCKINGHAM PALACE

Rain lashed at the gray-green walls of fabled Glamis Castle the night Princess Margaret was born, as a freak summer storm vented its full fury on the calm of the quiet Scottish countryside.

Outside the castle gates a little group of women, their heads covered by shawls, waited patiently for news. Sudden claps of thunder were followed by jagged flashes of lightning that illuminated the fairy-tale turrets of the castle and revealed anxiety on the faces of the women.

It was the twenty-first of August, 1930, a night when the eyes of Britain and all her peoples were centered on this obscure Scottish castle where they hoped a baby boy would be born.

The pretty Duchess of York, wife of Albert, second son of King George V and the indomitable Queen Mary, was expecting the arrival of her second child. Already they had one four-year-old daughter, Princess Elizabeth, and like everybody else they hoped for a boy. The Prince of Wales, heir to the throne, was then unmarried and the new baby, if a boy, would be third in succession to the throne.

Glamis Castle in the County of Angus had been the home of the Duchess of York's family since the fourteenth century. With the exception of Victoria Eugenie of Spain, the new baby was destined to be the first member of the royal family to be born north of the border since the ill-fated Charles I. Like Princess Margaret, he was always in hot water over something.

The Duke and Duchess of York were a very popular young couple. The Duchess, born Lady Elizabeth Bowes-Lyon, was five years younger than her husband and had been a childhood friend of his sister, Mary. A brunette with an exceptionally beautiful complexion, she was the ninth of ten children of the Earl and Countess of Strathmore.

When the Duke of York proposed marriage to his commoner bride (actually her Scottish ancestry was as royal as his own) his nervous stammer forced him to resort to a writing pad.

"She is a pretty and charming girl, and Bertie is a lucky fellow," declared King George V when he readily consented to the marriage.

The little girl from Glamis, who once had poured water on her father's guests from the castle battlements, found herself driving through cheering crowds to be married in historic Westminster Abbey. A Scottish fairy tale had really come true.

Here was a girl whose grandfather was a country clergyman, who could cook, sew and keep house, whose pictures never appeared in social gossip columns, marrying the King's second son. The man in the street was delighted with a marriage that had not been arranged to strengthen the dynasty.

To the Scottish women who had walked up the muddy road from Glamis village on that stormy August night, the Duchess of York was a local lass who had grown up and come home to have her baby. The southeast wing of the second floor was ablaze with lights, and at nine twenty-two in the evening the women's vigil was over, for news was brought them that the pretty Duchess had given birth to a nine-pound, eleven-ounce baby girl.

If her father was disappointed he didn't show it. His first thoughts were for the four-year-old Elizabeth who up to that time had been the pet of the whole family. How would she take the knowledge there was an interloper in the nest? As it turned out, Elizabeth took it very well.

Taking her by the hand, the Duke led the little girl into the nursery where her own cradle had been redecorated to accommodate the new baby. "I have a big surprise for you," he said. Then he lifted Elizabeth up to look in the cradle.

"Oh, it's a real baby!" she exclaimed, and from that day forward Elizabeth played almost a motherly role toward the new baby. She adored the child whose personality was destined to be so different from her own.

Wearing a rich ivory lace robe that had in turn been worn by three kings, the new baby was duly baptized Margaret Rose, a name that especially delighted the Scotts. Not only had she been born on the soil of their homeland, but she was also, they were sure, named for Saint Margaret, Queen of Scotland from 1046 to 1093.

However, she might well have been called after Queen Margaret of England, 1429-1481, who had distinguished herself by being sent to the Tower of London for five years.

The new baby, whose first name meant "a pearl," had inherited her mother's famed pink-and-white complexion, and had light brown hair and clear blue eyes. She was also the fourth in succession to the throne, with her sister Elizabeth taking precedence over her. Even as an infant she never seemed bothered by photographers. The first thing she remembers is falling out of her baby carriage.

At one year, Princess Margaret could say "Mummie" and "Papa" and she could also make more noise than the rest of the family put together. They wished the rumor mongers who declared she'd been born deaf and dumb could hear her. She tried hard to copy Elizabeth in everything and even today is a wonderful mimic.

When Margaret was three Sir James Barrie came to tea. A lover of children as only the author of *Peter Pan* could be, Sir James was intrigued with the baby Princess, who was then very much occupied opening her presents. He watched as she carefully examined a tiny doll's table complete with flower pots, then asked, "Is that really yours?"

Margaret looked up and said quite seriously, "It is mine and yours!"

This remark so pleased the author he decided to write it into *The Boy David,* his new play. He promised Margaret a penny royalty each time it was spoken on-stage. Four years later when Sir James lay on his deathbed he sent his secretary over to the little Princess with a bag full of pennies.

Always interested in people, Margaret once asked an astonished gentleman, "Are you an American?"

"No, I'm not," he answered, "but why do you ask?"

"Well, I see two gold teeth in your mouth," replied the observant little girl.

Margaret has one small recollection of her first party. A magician was to perform, so everybody tried to make her sit in the front row. She absolutely refused.

"But you'll see so much better," they said.

"I shall see too well," she replied.

Right from the first the Princess was a great dreamer. Her paternal grandfather, George V, was quite captivated by his youngest granddaughter although she lived a little in awe of him. This wasn't surprising, as his own children were never at ease with him.

Every morning at ten thirty Margaret would wave a handkerchief from a window at 145 Piccadilly and her grandfather would wave back from his window at Buckingham Palace. When he died she declared, "Grandpapa is in heaven now, and I am sure God finds him very useful."

She felt her Uncle David's (Edward VIII's) abdication much more deeply, for he always gave her Winnie-the-Pooh books. In all seriousness she asked, "Will they behead him?"

Margaret's home life at 145 Piccadilly was a happy one, almost like the life of any other well-to-do British child. She kept her thirty toy horses on the landing and enjoyed pillow fights with her father and sister Elizabeth. Her father could refuse his younger daughter nothing and Margaret made a habit of twisting him around her little finger. No matter how naughty she was—and she was very naughty at times—with a single quip she could melt anybody's anger and get her own way.

Once her mother dressed her as a Botticelli angel for a fancy-dress party but in spite of a halo she didn't fit the part.

"You don't quite look like an angel," observed the Duchess of York.

"All right," laughed Margaret, "then I'll have to go as a holy terror!"

At times the quieter Elizabeth was almost a martyr. Margaret resented the four years between them and couldn't see why protocol demanded that she take second place to her sister.

Elizabeth was long-suffering in most things, even when Margaret dropped salt in her tea and tapioca in her bath. At the time Elizabeth was presented with a lifesaving certificate for swimming, Margaret was furious. In front of everybody she picked up her sister's pet corgi dog, tossed him into the lake and, still wearing her best party dress, jumped in to rescue him.

On another occasion, feeling she merited more attention than she was getting, she rowed out to the middle of a pond and refused to come back.

Margaret was really a holy terror and her parents' guests came in for a fair share of her pranks. She was always hiding behind the draperies and jumping out at them. Three times in one morning she telephoned her father's secretary to go to his study and when the poor man arrived he found he wasn't needed.

Princess Elizabeth would explode with anger at Margaret's behavior but knew she had to put up with it. Once when her father remonstrated with her, Margaret listened to his scolding for a bit and then asked in her most serious voice, "Papa, do you sing 'God Save Thy Gracious Me'?"

The big move to the palace changed all their lives. They had loved Uncle David best of all the uncles and his going was a great wrench to them. He had always been so kind and understanding of children and once had even brought his week-end guests over from Fort Belvedere just to see his two small nieces keep house in Bwthyn Bach, the miniature cottage presented to Elizabeth by the people of Wales.

On December 30, 1936, the day of the abdication, when all the world was talking of that same Uncle David and his love for the twice-divorced Wallis Warfield Simpson, the two little girls stood on tiptoe to look at the crowds gathered in front of their house.

When told they were going to live in Buckingham

Palace, which has often been likened to camping in a museum, Elizabeth shook her head with horror and asked, "What! For always?"

Margaret's remark was of a more personal nature. She simply said, "Bother! Just when I had learned to write Margaret Rose of York. Now that Papa is King, I am nothing!"

Gone were the happy days when Elizabeth and Margaret played with their father in Hamilton Gardens. No longer was the London crowd able to peep through the iron railings and see the children romp and shout.

For the coronation of their parents the two princesses wore long white dresses with bows down the front, purple robes edged with ermine, and miniature golden coronets. They rode to Westminster Abbey in a real State coach and then, with their grandmother, Queen Mary, to look after them, had a wonderful time watching "Mummie and Papa in fancy dress" down below. Margaret fidgeted at times during the long ceremonial but on the whole she was remarkably good.

Queen Mary taught both children how to get used to crowds so that even their quiet father remarked how fearless his children seemed when they were watched by hundreds of people. As a boy, he had been petrified.

Margaret has since said, "It's strange, you know, but somehow, right from the beginning, I don't seem to remember noticing . . ."

There were other red-letter days in Margaret's young life. On November 6, 1935, she was bridesmaid to the Lady Alice Montagu-Douglas Scott at her marriage to the Duke of Gloucester (Uncle Harry). Margaret was most upset: because of the death of the bride's father the wedding wasn't held in Westminster Abbey as had been planned. Instead, the five-year-old girl had to be content with the Chapel Royal in Buckingham Palace.

Then there was that wonderful trip on the underground to the Y.W.C.A. in Tottenham Court Road, when Margaret took out her purse and for the first time paid her own fare. Elizabeth received a shilling a week pocket money but it was some years before Margaret was to get a similar allowance. Never mind—when the occasion arose she could always inveigle half-a-crown out of Alah, her nanny.

On vacation in Scotland Margaret loved to watch the Aberdeen Fish Express pass through Glamis Station. With Elizabeth she bought gum from a slot machine, stretched it across the rails and squealed with delight when a train passed over it.

At ten years she became interested in men. Her first crush was a palace footman, and she shocked her family —and the young man, too—by loudly announcing she thought he was handsome.

A lover of animals, she has never been without them nearby. She learned to ride a horse astride (though she can ride sidesaddle equally as well) and many were the happy hours she spent enjoying this pastime with her father and sister in Windsor's Great Park.

One pet, a Tibetan lion hound, was called Ching, and there was also a chameleon named Caspar. Margaret kept Caspar in a cage and worried a lot because often he was too lazy to eat. On visits to the zoo, Jacko the chimp was a very special friend.

When the Seventh Westminster Company of Girl Guides was specially formed for Princess Elizabeth and the daughters of Buckingham Palace personnel, Margaret was too young to join. This was a great blow to the youngster's pride, but she finally got in by signing up as a Brownie.

She developed a fashion sense early, criticized her own clothes and those of her mother, and made a vow that when she grew up, in matters of dress she'd copy her Aunt Marina, the beautiful Duchess of Kent, fashion-plate of the royal family.

Margaret hated being dressed in outfits identical to those worn by Elizabeth. During the grim days of World War II when clothing was rationed, her sister often dutifully wore clothes remodeled from their mother's. However, when it came Margaret's turn to inherit these hand-me-downs she absolutely refused them!

Chapter Two

GRANNIE ENGLAND

When Princess Margaret was one year old, one day she decided to hum the "Merry Widow Waltz." This quite upset her maternal grandmother, the Countess of Strathmore, who nearly dropped her. But it was Margaret's other grandmother, Queen Mary, or Grannie England, who had most to do with her upbringing.

"There are things children should see," declared Grannie England, and on fine afternoons when there were no royal duties to perform she would arrive in her old-fashioned Daimler to take Margaret and Elizabeth out.

Queen Mary believed that being royalty was no excuse for having bad manners. She was equally determined that her grandchildren should visit all of

London's best-known landmarks, for she had been born in the city, and she was especially proud of the fact.

She took them to see everything from the Zoological Gardens to St. Paul's Cathedral. Grannie England never got tired; she liked to see everything and when they were visiting an antique shop she would poke under the counter with her umbrella to see if anything was hidden there. She taught Elizabeth and Margaret how to recognize a good piece of furniture, and it was from her that Margaret developed a love of antique furnishings, especially Sheraton.

On the death of George V, Queen Mary had retired to historic Marlborough House where she lived in the midst of fellow-Londoners who regarded her as their neighbor and friend, surrounded by her art collections, refusing ever to answer personally a telephone (which she hated).

Speaking of Grannie England, Sir Winston Churchill has said: "Queen Mary did not cling to the insubstantial shadows of what had been. She moved easily through the changing scenes. New ideas held no terrors for her. Dispassionate in judgment, practical in all things, she was also far too much interested in the present to be unduly prejudiced by the past."

She was the power behind her husband, who more than once said of her great knowledge of current events, "I don't know how she does it."

She was not above prodding him with her old-fashioned silk parasol when the speech he was delivering was too long-winded, and whispering in his ear, "Now, George, that's enough."

Grannie England's so-called "retirement" in 1936 will go down in history as one of the busiest on record. She promptly moved into Marlborough House, where she employed forty-seven servants.

Elizabeth and Margaret were frequent visitors to the establishment, which was almost more royal than the palace itself. The quiet, dutiful Elizabeth was a child after the old Queen's heart. She also loved Margaret although at times she found her hard to understand. In later years when Margaret's night-club appearances made popular copy in the morning newspapers, Grannie England always wrote her a personal reprimand.

Both children adored this grandmother who rose every morning at seven-thirty sharp and washed from a silver sink which was hand-filled, simply because she felt modern plumbing disfigured her bedroom.

They knew that their grandmother wouldn't change her ways for anybody, that she always dressed completely for breakfast and personally arranged her high hair-do. She always took great interest in answering her own mail and advised them that when they grew up they should do the same, discarding only letters from professional beggars and crackpots—both of which she herself could spot instantly.

She hated to waste time. If she was working at her embroidery or riding in a car she always had somebody read the newspapers aloud to her. She enjoyed reading murder mysteries and hated to have plays censored as unfit for her royal eyes.

Always hovering in the background during the Princesses' schooldays, she came up with several down-to-earth suggestions. She was against Elizabeth and Margaret's learning so much arithmetic, for she declared they would not need it. She advocated more religion and history, which she was sure they'd need, and poetry— always poetry—because it was good memory training for the busy days ahead.

Queen Mary's concept of a princess's life was unlike most people's. She made sure that her granddaughters were taught to cook, clean their own rooms and darn their own stockings. She encouraged them to buy materials at the local branch of Woolworth's and make their own Christmas presents.

Popular with the poor, as Princess Margaret is today, Queen Mary always did her best to better their conditions. Once she upset a society committee by refusing to visit some model apartments they were sponsoring, by-passing them for a group of slum dwellings next door.

Afterwards she declared, "These houses are a disgrace to the country and an outrage to the poor souls who live in them. I shall come here again, and if nothing is done I shall withdraw my name from your list of patrons." In a short time the houses had all been rebuilt.

One of the nicest stories about her—and incidentally one of Princess Margaret's favorites—concerns the naming of the ocean liner, the *Queen Mary*, September 26, 1934.

The Cunard Line's directors had decided to name the vessel *Victoria* in line with the company tradition of using names ending in "-ia." Then they went about asking Queen Mary to christen the ship. Sir Percy Bates, chairman of the Cunard Line, called on King George V and told him of their decision to name the new ship "after one of Britain's most noble queens."

"Oh," exclaimed the King beaming with pleasure, "Her Majesty will be pleased."

For the rest of his life he never knew he had named the *Queen Mary*. The secret was equally well kept until after the death of his wife.

"Proper poise begins with your feet," Grannie England instructed Princess Margaret, and even today she prefers the open-toed shoes recommended by her grandmother. As well as being justly proud of her tiny, size 2½ shoes, she insists on designs that are easy on the feet as well as elegant.

Queen Mary never forgot the domestic crisis that occurred when Margaret was a teen-ager and her mother found a favorite fox cape missing. Later she learned that her younger daughter had borrowed it for the evening. When Queen Mary died she willed Margaret a dark Canadian mink coat. Today the princess is still wearing it—remodeled of course.

Perhaps the most important thing Grannie England taught her granddaughter was the way to an Englishman's heart. She taught her how to make a good cup of tea!

Chapter Three

SCHOOLDAYS

For seventeen years Elizabeth and Margaret were taught by a governess, Miss Marion Crawford, whom they affectionately nicknamed, Crawfie. Miss Crawford was a pleasant, even-tempered Scotswoman. She held a Bachelor of Arts degree from Edinburgh University.

Margaret had little difficulty with her lessons. She seemed to absorb everything like a sponge and at all times was mercurial and carefree.

Both children followed a regular schoolroom curriculum which was carefully superintended by Queen Mary. Crawfie did most of the teaching, although specialists in certain subjects were called in. Canon Crawley, a member of the Chapter of St. George's Chapel, Windsor, instructed them in Scripture. Margaret has to thank the

Viscomtesse de Bellaigue for teaching her to speak fluent French with hardly a trace of accent.

With the outbreak of World War II the little Princess found herself one of the many thousands of évacuées. She was sent off to Windsor with Elizabeth and saw her parents only during the week-ends. Lessons went on as usual; the royal sisters had their own Dig For Victory garden, where they grew carrots, lettuces and onions. The highlights of these grim years were the Christmas pantomimes which they helped write, perform and produce.

The most elaborate of these was staged at Windsor Castle, December 19, 1941, when even the King and Queen were drafted to help with the writing.

The pantomime was *Cinderella*, with Princess Margaret playing the title role. Many people have said since what a wonderful career Margaret could have had as an actress—or even as a writer of children's stories—if she had not been born a princess.

Princess Elizabeth played Prince Florizel and in one scene wore knickerbockers. H. I. Tannar, a local schoolmaster, was the producer and also portrayed the Wicked Baron. The cast was made up of twenty-four children including, besides the Princesses, a gardener's daughter, the bright-eyed son of the King's page, and some London évacuées.

For days before, the children came to Windsor Castle to rehearse and work on costumes and props. Margaret and Elizabeth were delighted and at week-ends had heaps of new things to relate to their visiting parents. For the first time they were really meeting children from the outside world; to the two children who up to that time had led almost cloistered lives, it was a memorable and an unforgettable experience.

When the great day for the performance arrived, the King and Queen were among the audience. Margaret, who had been so naughty clowning at rehearsals, stole the show, especially during one big scene which she shared with Cyril Woods, son of a motor mechanic, and Uncle Remus, a large white rabbit.

Among the youngsters the girls met during their early years was fair-haired Prince Philip of Greece. However, according to the records, it was not until 1939 that they had an encounter of any importance.

That year, George VI took Elizabeth and Margaret on a tour of inspection of the Royal Naval College at Dartmouth. Prince Philip, five years older than Elizabeth, was detailed to entertain the Princesses. Elizabeth later confided to her parents that she thought him a show-off, but the more impressionable Margaret declared he was "smashing."

Toward the close of the war Elizabeth joined the army and Margaret was more or less left on her own. At fourteen, she was caught sampling a bottle of champagne; at sixteen, she was using Schiaparelli's "Shocking." When her father asked her not to drink any more sherry at a party, she retorted, "If you don't let me have another glass I won't launch your old ships for you."

Another time he demanded to know where she had ever learned such language, and then came the answer Margaret now wishes everybody would forget, "Oh, at my mother's knee—or some such low joint."

She walked in on most of Elizabeth's teen-age parties and deliberately stole the show from her quieter sister. It took a long time for Elizabeth to put her foot down and then it was only to be told, "You can go and look after your Empire: I can look after myself!"

When her mother sadly shook her head, Margaret gave one of her stone-melting smiles and said very sweetly, "Oh, Mummie, isn't it lucky that Lilibet's the elder?"

At seventeen Britain's "Dresden China Princess" took a course in constitutional history, left on the royal tour of South Africa with her parents and sister, and never again returned to her old classroom timetable. Crawfie came to the palace for some time to instruct Margaret in special subjects that interested her but, with Elizabeth's wedding to Philip, Margaret was thrown into the limelight and her official studies came to an end.

Chapter Four

ENTER PRINCE PHILIP

Princess Margaret has described her brother-in-law Philip as "the big brother I really needed when I was younger, to keep me in order."

She constantly consults him on matters of interest that take place outside the palace and they discuss politics and affairs of state together.

Often she has complained to Philip that "men have a much better time" and then teased him about his cricket and polo playing. When staying at the Balmoral estate in Scotland she hates to accompany Elizabeth deer-stalking or the Queen Mother fishing. At such times she often drives over the moors to join Philip and the other members of his party for a picnic lunch. Princess Margaret prefers masculine company.

At times Margaret shares her own private jokes with Philip, and Elizabeth has been known to reprimand them. She has never forgotten their childhood days when she felt it her sisterly duty to say, "Margaret, if you see someone wearing a funny hat, you are not to point."

Philip has been the one most responsible for encouraging Margaret to drive her own car and, in spite of some of the Queen's subjects who would like to wrap them both in cotton wool, she has gone ahead and done so. Philip's own driving history hasn't been perfect. Just for the record, in 1957 he bumped a taxi in May and banged up another car in June.

Even Margaret's driving lessons with her brother-in-law could not be private. When they were out alone in his long, low, hundred-mile-an-hour sports car, their course across the countryside was being carefully plotted by the police.

The day Princess Elizabeth married Lieutenant Philip Mountbatten (formerly Prince Philip of Greece) in Westminister Abbey the life of each member of Britain's first family changed for the better.

Philip was the only boy friend Elizabeth ever had. Like Margaret he was her absolute opposite in make-up. Perhaps that was why he attracted her so much.

The King had always wanted a son and, although he hated the thought of having his daughter grow up and leave him, in time he became very much attached to his son-in-law.

As for Margaret, she had always liked Philip. They spoke the same language and enjoyed the same jokes, and at times he could be just as different and unconventional as she. It was nice to have somebody like him in the family, although he also had to learn to temper his natural sense of humor.

Like Margaret, he rebelled against certain aspects of court protocol. In order to conform he donned a kilt at Balmoral but told close friends he felt a bit of a fool to be wearing it. He hated bowler hats and for a long while refused to be seen in one. Then, too, his Bohemian tastes in some things worried the older court advisers. He drove fast cars and they never quite knew what he was going to say next. One problem child like Margaret was enough for any royal family, but Elizabeth had made up her mind and, like dear old Grannie England, at times she could be really stubborn.

Elizabeth had exchanged long letters with Philip while he, then a young officer in the Royal Navy, was at sea, and on his shore furloughs he'd become a frequent visitor at Buckingham Palace. The budding romance was not a secret for long. Many Britishers considered Philip a foreigner—he was through fate a Greek prince, although nobody could be more British in his yearnings than he. Questions were asked in Parliament, and Elizabeth became nervous and unhappy.

Margaret was especially sympathetic to her sister during those trying days, something Elizabeth tried to remember at the time of the furor over Peter Townsend. Once she remarked, "Poor Lilibet—not even a romance of her own."

Elizabeth's life had always been sheltered, whereas Philip had spent most of his childhood in boarding schools. His naval training and active wartime duties as a sailor had made him familiar with the lot of the common man. In Australia he had made many friends, and in the United States also. Some of the guests Philip invited to his wedding were certainly not in the Buckingham Palace social register.

During their separation, when Elizabeth was touring South Africa with her parents and sister, she was melancholy and listless. Meanwhile, things were happening at home to speed an early engagement. Philip renounced his title of prince, became a naturalized British subject and adopted the name Philip Mountbatten.

Philip's background is an interesting one. Both he and his wife are great-great-grandchildren of Queen Victoria. His ancestry is that of a Dane of the royal house of Schleswig-Holstein-Sonderburg, yet he was born a Greek.

His grandfather, Prince William of Denmark, was made King of the Hellenes in 1863, formally taking the title of George I, of Greece. Philip, who was born on the Island of Corfu, June 10, 1921, is the only son of the late Prince Andrew, fourth son of George I, and of Alice, daughter of the first Marquess of Milford Haven.

Philip's mother has now become a member of a religious order and spends her life in the gray habit of a nun, working among the people on the Aegean Island of Tinos. During World War II she did heroic work with the Red Cross in Greece. She attended her son's wedding to Elizabeth, but not the funeral of his father-in-law, George VI. At the time she told reporters that her work must come first.

Following the revolution in Greece that cost Philip's uncle his throne, Prince Andrew and his family went into exile and settled in Paris. His mother ran an art store there and the boy Philip spent his early years visiting more fortunate relatives. Later he was sent to Britain to be looked after by Lady Milford Haven, his grandmother, and Lord Louis Mountbatten, his uncle. The latter, an officer in the Royal Navy, became Philip's idol.

Philip first attended a British preparatory school before being sent to Dr. Kurt Hahn's progressive school in Germany. There he was brought up under Spartan conditions, and flourished under them. A year later his German relatives, embarrassed because he made fun of the Nazis (Philip's four sisters had all wed German royalty), sent him back to Britain.

In 1934 Dr. Hahn, by then in disfavor himself with Hitler, fled to Scotland and reopened his school at Gordonstoun. Philip once more became his pupil. Often visitors to the area would ask school officials, "Which one is the prince?"

The answer would be, "That one," and the visitors would be surprised to see a handsome youngster, covered with grease, at work on a boat engine.

In 1940 Philip, now a midshipman, commenced five years of naval service at sea, serving on H.M.S. *Valiant* where he was mentioned in dispatches for good work during the battle of Cape Matapan. He saw duty in other spheres and finally became a first lieutenant aboard a destroyer in the Pacific, serving as aide-de-camp to Lord Louis Mountbatten who was now Supreme Allied Commander in the South-East Asia Command.

Shortly after Elizabeth's return to London they were

married. Their wedding November 20, 1947, brought a ray of sunshine to postwar Britain. Margaret was a bit peeved at having to walk with her young cousin, Princess Alexandra of Kent, who was then a gawky schoolgirl, but after the reception, when Elizabeth and Philip were leaving for their honeymoon, she was out in the London crowd pelting them with rice.

For once Margaret's actions were not criticized. As one member of the press remarked, "Well, it could only happen in England."

Chapter Five

THE GRAND TOUR

In the spring of 1949 Princess Margaret made the Grand Tour. She visited Naples, Capri, Rome, Florence, Venice and Paris. She also gained her wings as a full-fledged adult member of the British royal family.

Not that it was the first time she had gone abroad on her own. On September 6, 1948 she had undertaken a special mission on behalf of the royal family by going to the Netherlands and representing them at the enthronement of Queen Juliana. On that occasion she received the Grand Cross of the Order of the Netherlands Lion from the Dutch Queen. In her official party, looking handsome in his blue air force uniform, was Group-Captain Peter Townsend.

King George and his Scottish wife showed good common sense when they allowed their younger daughter to take a vacation alone—that is, without some senior member of the family tagging along as chaperone. Even well-behaved Elizabeth had never made such a trip as the one allotted to Margaret. She had visited Canada, but had her new husband to help and advise her.

Before Margaret was safely home again in the cloistered walls of Buckingham Palace, she was to cause many eyelids to flutter. She was soundly censured by certain Protestant organizations for visiting the Pope, and criticized by staid British dowagers for wearing a bathing suit.

The romantic Italians had expected a fairy princess and they got her. Margaret was completely their cup of tea, for they found her just what a well-brought-up young girl should be.

In spite of the reports in some European newspapers, the Italians did not pester or mob her. In Naples her arrival was hardly noticed by the people and when she appeared they politely clapped their hands.

They waited until Margaret went sailing in her small motor yacht; then boatloads of the famed fishermen of Sorrento made it their business to serenade her—and Margaret loved it.

In Florence she was formally welcomed by the mayor, Signor Fabiani, and his wife who gave her a bouquet. Then they showed the delighted Princess over the Palazzo Vecchio, which for centuries was the center of the civic life of the city. The mayor gave her a fifteenth-century plaque and later she signed the Book of Honor, which also bore the signature of her great-great-grandmother, Queen Victoria.

She visited the Basilica of San Lorenzo and gasped over the sculptures of Michelangelo. Then at the Teatro Comunale, the Florence Opera House, Margaret won the hearts of all the Florentines. Wildly applauding the performance, she did not rush for the exit as soon as it was over. Instead she stopped to applaud some more!

Buckingham Palace officials sedately made the announcement that "the Princess is getting experience at first hand of various aspects of the national life to fit herself for an adult role as a member of the Royal Family" but even this explanation did not help the outburst both before and after her visit to Pope Pius XII. Not that she was creating a precedent by calling on the Pontiff for when her grandparents, King George V and Queen Mary, had visited the Vatican in 1923 they had touched off a mass protest meeting in London's Albert Hall.

A spokesman for the Protestant Truth Society said quite bluntly: "When Princess Margaret sees the Pope she will be directly evading that point in the bill which lays down that no member of Britain's Royal Family must hold communion with the Holy See of the Church of Rome."

Nevertheless, Margaret donned a neat black dress and a long velvet cloak and, with a mantilla on her head, called on the Pope to spend twenty minutes in lively conversation with him. The Pope was much impressed with the Princess and presented her with a painting of the Virgin Mary.

Back in Britain there were more protests. Although the Archbishop of Canterbury, spiritual head of the

Church of England, made no comment at all, others more than made up for his silence.

The Reverend Donald M'Kenzie of Oban, Scotland, speaking at the Free Church Assembly, submitted a report to the Committee on Public Questions, Religion and Morals with the stinging statement: "We deprecate and deplore visits to the Vatican by those in high places which have taken place in recent weeks."

The Executive Committee of the National Union of Protestants were so upset they sent a telegram to Margaret's father (one of the most God-fearing kings who ever sat on the British throne) which read: "Many thousands of Your Majesty's most loyal Protestant subjects are greatly incensed at the visit of Princess Margaret to the Pope."

Yet, in spite of the uproar, Margaret went right on enjoying her holiday. She visited the Forum and the Palatine, studied new excavations of an early Roman settlement, went to the International Horse Show and attended divine service twice—at St. Mark's in the Via Maggio and All Saints in the Via del Babuino—both Anglican churches.

On the Isle of Capri Margaret took note of some advice given her in the Rome newspaper, *Giornale d'Italia:* "If the Princess wants to learn about Italy and the Italian people she'll have to do better than this. All she's been seeing are fronts and backs of police agents."

Margaret's bodyguard up to then had consisted of two Scotland Yard detectives and six Italian plain-clothes men. They accompanied her everywhere and even told newspaper cameramen when they might take pictures.

Then Margaret put her foot down and decided to do a "Garbo." She asked to be alone, although this was almost impossible on an island as small as Capri. The local people did their best to grant her wish and, dressed in a modest swimsuit, she tried to "disappear" for the afternoon.

However the newspaper photographers were not so cooperative, and with the use of special telephoto lenses photographed the mermaid princess from a spot five hundred yards away.

Margaret who is a good swimmer—later in the West Indies she became the first member of Britain's royal family to dabble in snorkel underwater swimming—looked very shapely in her beach attire, which isn't surprising for one whose figure has been said to rival that of Marilyn Monroe.

Back in England the telephoto pictures caused another outburst of indignation, but Margaret only laughed.

The Princess enjoyed Capri more than any other place she visited. It was a new experience to send a hotel bellboy down to buy you a straw sun hat, to wear dark glasses in public and explore quaint shops laden with bric-a-brac. It was fun to eat with other guests in a hotel dining room—even if it meant pretending nobody was watching you. In any case, Margaret has never been accused of being self-conscious. She was not pestered by the curious as much as some people thought. And as for the press—in spite of the bathing suit incident—they behaved themselves well and she thanked them publicly.

At the luxurious new Caesar Augustus Hotel, built high up at Anacapri, she attended a special tea dance in her honor. Her feet must have been aching from all the walking she'd been doing, for even the sambas played by the three-piece band couldn't persuade her to dance. Instead she beat time to the music with her foot and sat demurely sipping a glass of orange juice.

In Switzerland she received another warm welcome and again asked for a smaller police escort, as she wanted to do some private shopping. She'd heard about Lausanne and the luxury stores that lined its main thoroughfare so, accompanied by ex-Queen Victoria Eugenie of Spain at whose villa she spent the night, the Princess went shopping.

In one large store Margaret had a chance meeting with ex-King Michael of Rumania and shook hands with him. She purchased a box of chocolates and Victoria Eugenie bought her a small square watch with a brown silk strap. At midnight she caught the train for Paris.

In Paris, after requesting privacy, Margaret drove off to the sanctuary of the British Embassy. Later she visited the Elysée Palace, the Presidential residence, to have lunch with Mme. Vincent Auriol, wife of the President.

In spite of the informal nature of her visit, the French were not disappointed—they liked royalty that was not their own—and in her five-day visit Princess Margaret captured their hearts. She captured the headlines too; even the Communist *Ce Soir* published a three-column photograph of her arrival at the railway terminal.

Being Princess Margaret, and since this was Paris, she made it her business to visit three of the biggest fashion salons in the city.

Wearing dove-gray, she arrived at the gilt salon of Jean Desses, dressmaker for her favorite aunt, the Duchess of Kent, to attend the afternoon show, and watched a hundred and fifty models display clothing that ranged from black silk beach slacks to gold satin evening gowns.

At Christian Dior's, the staff just had time to fill the vases with fresh pink roses in honor of her visit. Movie stars Marlene Dietrich, the late Maria Montez and Norma Shearer were other visitors. Margaret, who wore a rose-colored raw silk suit for the occasion, was described by an onlooker as being "fresh, young and pretty."

Wearing a Molyneux dress, she dropped in at the Molyneux Salon with a pompon hat and ankle-strap shoes. Twenty-five excited models paraded before her and Margaret was charmed with a red satin faille sheath gown.

The Grand Tour gave Princess Margaret confidence. Her sister Elizabeth had never undertaken such a private journey on her own, and in any case she would now always have Philip to share her royal travels. Margaret's, until such time as she also married, would have to be undertaken alone.

Margaret's informal travels through Italy and France, her friendly calls on the Pope and the French President's wife, were good lessons for her in dealing with people. The Grand Tour was in a way a royal experiment and in spite of the bathing suit incident it was a successful one.

When she flew back to London Airport, heading the reception committee was Wing Commander Peter Townsend, Equerry to the King.

Chapter Six

CHARLEY'S AUNT

"Now I suppose they'll call me Charley's Aunt," laughed Princess Margaret when she first heard the news of the birth of Prince Charles, her nephew, November 14, 1948.

Charley's Aunt or Princess Margaret, she had at last achieved her lifelong ambition to grow up. No longer was she to be the little sister; she was very much of a person in her own right.

The year 1949 was destined to be one of the most important in her career as a princess. As her father said, "Margaret can charm the pearl out of an oyster." And now she set out to do just that to his subjects.

Actually she had undertaken her first public engagement alone a little before Elizabeth's marriage and had succeeded in capturing the hearts of a Belfast crowd by handing a young dock hand a rose from her bouquet. After that she polished off a launching by giving her first luncheon speech in a confident, unaffected voice without glancing once at the script. Some of the officials felt quite uncomfortable and wished that she had made at least one small mistake. It didn't seem possible that this was the same girl who got slightly bored at times on the long South African tour.

Years before she had made the childhood remark, "I wish we could be visiting these places when royalty aren't." She had inherited her lovable inquisitiveness from Grannie England.

In March she journeyed to Bristol to open a "Youth at Work and at Leisure" exhibition and the Bristol School of Nursing. At the Bristol Royal Infirmary she signed the visitors' book with a pen used by her grandparents, George and Mary, thirty-seven years before.

To the young nurses Margaret said: "I feel that there are many girls of my age who would, like you, find a full and happy life in a career of nursing. Indeed, the unselfish desire to aid the sick and suffering is a deep instinct in many women. It requires exceptional qualities in those who choose it, vision to guide their choice, courage to learn, determination to endure and pride in achievement."

She visited Denham Film Studios to see how motion pictures are made; went to Kemsley House and watched the *Daily Graphic* put to bed; and, dressed solemnly in dove-gray, arrived at the Royal Courts of Justice to listen to an action for damages in an alleged slander, assault, battery and false-imprisonment case.

These various activities, repetitious as they must sound, were an important steppingstone in the training Margaret was getting as a career princess.

The endless round of hospital visiting, bazaar open-ing and stone-laying ceremonies provided an excellent source of training for the weeks-long tours she is now called on to take as a good-will ambassador and personal representative for her sister, the Queen.

Just as learning poetry for memory training, as recom-mended by Grannie England, was sound help in re-calling strings of names, so were these earlier public engagements good proving ground for Margaret's far-flung tours of the future.

It should also be remembered that Princess Margaret is a working princess and that what may seem like sheer fun to the traditional shop girl, in reality is back-break-ing work. For the reader who wants to find out for him-self: shake hands and try to say something different to five hundred different people. It's harder than you think!

In a cherry-red outfit she delighted 550 men at a party for wounded ex-servicemen and listened with pride when Sir Louis Greig said she "gave a little glamour to a drab world." Britain in particular was feeling more than a little drab after years of rationing, bombing and gener-ally "going without." American and Canadian service-men stationed in that theater of World War II were only too familiar with the sacrifices made by the inhabitants of the embattled island.

With the ending of hostilities rationing continued and the people were called on to help win the post-war battle for survival.

One of the bright spots of this period was Princess Margaret, who went about charming the hearts of her father's subjects just in the same way as he had once said she could charm the pearl out of an oyster.

London's dowagers, however, continued to shake their heads every time they read in the newspapers that Princess Margaret had danced until early morning in one of London's fashionable night clubs. It was bad enough, they thought, when Margaret danced the can-can at the home of Sharman Douglas, daughter of the American Ambassador, although they never stopped to consider that seven other young ladies were also included in the act; that Margaret's mother had given permission; and that Princess Elizabeth, dressed as a parlormaid, was present with her Philip made up as the butler.

The dowagers complained that thirty years ago all this would never have happened; that in those days the King's younger daughter would have attended select private balls in Kensington Palace or at stately houses in Park Lane.

But the poor old dears were in for another shocker. At a Hallowe'en charity ball Princess Margaret calmly took out a cigarette and lighted it in public. In so doing she made world headlines as the first female member of Britain's royal family to smoke in public. Such a thing was unthinkable to members of the old school; at least Grannie England had the decency to smoke in private and, after all, she had acquired the habit from her black sheep, the Duke of Windsor.

As far back as Tudor days when Sir Walter Raleigh encouraged Elizabeth I to take a puff of tobacco, smoking had been taboo among Britain's royal ladies, for the

Virgin Queen hadn't liked it. Even her successor, James I, son of Mary Queen of Scots, dismissed smoking as a "filthie novelty."

Britain's masses, reading of sinful Margaret in their morning newspapers, took it as further proof that she was just a normal girl, though some did remark that with cigarettes priced at forty-nine cents a pack only a princess could afford them.

Since then Margaret and her long, jeweled cigarette holders have won popular approval, and consequently the cigarette holder trade has increased enormously.

Margaret celebrated her nineteenth birthday in the castle where she was born, and many of the older Scots recalled the local tradition that a girl-child born at Glamis would be wed before she was twenty.

For the first time Prince Charles attended his Aunt Margo's birthday. Another guest was the thirteen-year-old Duke of Kent, eldest son of her Aunt Marina. Today the young Duke is as high spirited as Margaret ever was.

To a group of Presbyterian Church elders Margaret sang, "I'm Just a Girl Who Can't Say No"—and they liked it. Then for other guests she gave her own impersonation of Danny Kaye, which she rounded off by singing, "Baby, It's Cold Outside."

The King, after watching her performance with natural fatherly pride, sighed, and said rather wistfully, "She has so much talent—and it must, necessarily, go to waste!"

Chapter Seven

COMING OF AGE

Although the old prophecy did not come true and Princess Margaret was still very much a spinster on her twentieth birthday, this did not in any way stop the good-natured Scots from helping to celebrate her coming-of-age the following year at Balmoral.

As a royal personage officially comes of age at eighteen, Margaret's twenty-first birthday was more of a family affair—made all the more intimate and wonderful by the spontaneous part that the Scottish countryfolk living in the vicinity of Balmoral took in it.

Before going up to Scotland for the great day Margaret attended a number of polo matches at Cowdray Park with Tom Egerton, a former captain in the Coldstream Guards with whom her name had been romantically linked by the press.

A South American barbecue given by the Argentine team was the highlight of the week for Margaret. She attended it with Billy Wallace, stepson of Herbert Agar, former Louisville, Kentucky, newspaper editor, and astounded even her hosts by the way she could dance the tango. At the barbecue, seven sheep were roasted whole.

She broke her journey to the land of the heather to attend the Cumberland Pageant at Carlisle, mingling freely with ten thousand people in the audience. The pageant depicted, among other historical episodes, the tragic story of the much-married Mary Queen of Scots who was beheaded by the first Queen Elizabeth.

The grouse shooting season was due to open when the Princess eventually reached Balmoral, the royal retreat so popular with Victoria and Albert.

Although beloved by the royal pair as their "dear paradise," Balmoral, built from Albert's own design in 1855, is a jumble of German turrets and pseudo-Scottish architecture. It replaced the beautiful Balmoral House which was torn down. The forests surrounding their dream palace nostalgically reminded Albert of his native Germany.

Long before Margaret was awake on her birthday morning, greetings from all parts of the world were arriving at the castle and the secretarial staff was kept busy answering them. Later a red mail truck made its way up the long winding road, loaded with cards, letters and gifts from well-wishers living in all parts of the British Empire and friends across the world.

Her parents presented Margaret with a green Daimler roadster which, with the sales tax, costs about three thousand pounds ($8,400). Princess Elizabeth gave her sister a necklace made of Persian-mined turquoises with diamond and turquoise earrings to match.

The staff at Balmoral had each contributed the sum of half a crown—about thirty-five cents—to purchase Margaret an antique writing cabinet and table for her birthday. The staff at Sandringham, country estate of the royal family in Norfolk, gave her a silver cigarette box—positive proof that they did not disapprove of her smoking! The Sandringham tenants, where her father was loved more as the village squire than King of England, bought her a racing bag fitted to hold a pair of binoculars.

King George VI, who liked to shoot grouse as much as he liked to eat them, took off for a shooting expedition during the morning. Later in the day his wife and daughters joined him for a picnic lunch. There on the open moor the king proposed the health of the younger daughter he'd often told not to be "so damned cheeky."

Princess Margaret had never looked more beautiful than she did that day in her simple tweed jacket, Scottish kilt and bright headscarf. Sitting among the heather, her mother was proud and happy that Margaret's birthplace had been her own beloved Scotland.

In the afternoon Princess Elizabeth's youngsters, Prince Charles, and flaxen-haired Princess Anne who had been born the previous year, arrived from nearby Birkhall for tea. They had been promised that if they were good they should stay and help Aunt Margo blow out the twenty-one candles on her gigantic birthday cake.

At dinner that evening nobody in the royal dining hall outshone the birthday Princess who was radiantly gowned in a Dior creation of sheer organza. As a special surprise, the King had arranged for five kilted pipers led by Pipe Major J. MacDonald to march into the hall and play all her favorite Scottish airs, for both Margaret and Elizabeth particularly love Scottish music.

Then the guests gathered on the lawn and watched the lighting of a huge bonfire built by estate workers in honor of their own princess. As it blazed away on the mountainside high above the castle, Margaret was visibly touched by the loyal friendship shown her by the Scottish countryfolk, her "ain people."

Just a week later her father left Balmoral for London. Although he did not then know it, he was gravely ill with a lung ailment. His wife, elder daughter and son-in-law also returned to London as soon as they were informed how sick he really was.

At her father's express wish, Margaret remained at Balmoral and acted as the perfect hostess for the family guests. What anxiety she suffered while going about her duties only Margaret knows, for she loved her father more than anybody else.

Margaret flew to London when her beloved Papa underwent his serious lung operation, staying with her mother to comfort and give strength during the critical days that followed. A week later the King was making such a splendid recovery he insisted she return to his grandchildren in Scotland.

Chapter Eight

MEN, MONEY BUT NO DIAMOND RING

Speculation as to whom Princess Margaret would marry was a common subject in the daily press during 1951. She was linked romantically with Billy Wallace and during that season attended the major social events with him.

She sat and watched as he played polo at Cowdray Park in Sussex and later, when his team won, presented him with a trophy. Then she went to stay with his family, where she was intrigued by the "simple domesticity" of their ten-room house which was run by only three servants and a gardener. The American press reported that by upper-class British standards this was somewhat roughing it.

Handsome Billy was the sole heir to a million pounds ($2,800,000) left him by his father, Evan Wallace, in

[56]

1941. One newspaper declared the Princess was "going domestic" and that during her stay with the Agars she wore the same dress three days running.

Londoners speculated too over another supposed romance, this time with the tall red-haired Earl of Dalkeith, twenty-eight, son of the Duke and Duchess of Buccleuch and a godson of Queen Mary.

Buckingham Palace sources retorted tartly: "No comment" when asked if Margaret would wed Dalkeith. Excitement mounted when the Earl drove to Sandringham where the royal family were holding a house party. No engagement was announced and in due course the handsome earl wed somebody else.

Dashing Tom Egerton was still supposedly in the running for the most eligible spinster in England. She stayed with his parents and was seen in his company, but as usual it was only a rumor. People were beginning to shake their heads over Margaret and to call her a bit of a flirt.

In spite of this she continued to go dancing and was usually photographed with one of the guards officers. One terrified young man was asked to polka with her, but blushingly confessed, "I can't dance a polka, ma'am."

The Princess saw he was speaking the truth. "Neither could I," she told him, "until they forced me to learn it, so let's dance something to polka time."

For Margaret the year was a busy one and the ill-health of her father brought added burdens to the hard-worked royal family. She visited North Wales for the first time to attend the Annual Conference of the National Union of Teachers at Llandudno. Margaret charmed the teachers, but she was again in hot water with the powerful League Against Cruel Sports. They passed a strongly worded resolution that they had "read with regret that Princess Margaret followed a hunt of the Pytchley Foxhounds on January 6 in a motor vehicle."

Further it complained: "The Princess cannot be aware of the views which a very large number of British people hold about fox hunting. Had she been so aware we feel certain she would not have been present at an amusement which is regarded by quite half the people of Britain with absolute loathing and abhorrence, by reason of its inherent cruelty to the unfortunate animal involved."

The resolution did little good, for Margaret still goes hunting.

In spite of this kind of criticism she managed to keep her sense of humor and meet the spirit of the occasion. When she visited an exhibition of model houses at Olympia, her elevator jammed. To the officials present it was an awful moment but Margaret saw her opportunity for a few quips.

Turning to Jennifer Bevan, her lady in waiting, she asked, "Have you got the *sal volatile*, Jennifer?"

Then seeing a crowd of people watching them she laughed, "Look at all those glorious people staring at us without being able to help. Do you think we should yell or rattle the bars?"

By that time the officials in the elevator with the Princess were most upset and it didn't help any when Margaret spotted a food center.

"Oh good," she said to Jennifer Bevan. "If worst comes to worst they can always pass bits of food to us through the bars."

Then with mocking innocence she inquired, "Why don't we go to the top and start all over again?"

Needless to say the harassed officials could have throttled her.

With other members of her family she met the King and Queen of Denmark upon their arrival in London for a state visit, May 8, 1951, and from May 30 to June 4 accompanied her mother on a visit to Northern Ireland for the opening of Ulster's Festival of Britain exhibition. The ailing King was unable to go with them, and later on September 27 Margaret was to become one of the five Counselors of State appointed to act for him during his illness. Today if Queen Elizabeth is out of the country a similar council is formed with the Queen Mother and Margaret almost certainly forming part of it.

This should not be confused with what are called Margaret's "state duties." This means certain duties which she carries out as representative of the Queen, such as the opening of the new West Indies Legislature.

She made her most important speech of the year in March while addressing cadets as Commandant-in-Chief of the St. John Ambulance Brigade Cadet Movement when she noted: "It is not training alone, however, which yields great leaders. When we think of the men and women whose leadership in thought and deed has inspired our people through the centuries to their great achievements, we remember their exertions and example, their tolerance and good humor, their devotion and discipline, and above all, their lasting trust in God. It is with such high human qualities as these that our leaders of the future must be imbued."

She constantly referred to God in her speech. Already her interest in metaphysics and theology was growing. Today she is said to be the most religiously informed member of her family.

At Datchet, England, she was called a "good sport" when the canvas tent roof under which she was standing to sign a portrait of herself split and showered her with two gallons of rainwater. Her brand new hat and the painting were drenched but the Princess kept on smiling.

The London dress houses were doing a brisk business among the teen-agers and fashion-conscious women who were constantly demanding clothes "like Princess Margaret is wearing." The Apparel and Fashion Industry Association put out a statement saying: "The interest they take in their clothes increases the interest of the public—not only in Britain but overseas. We are fortunate to have two such fashion-conscious princesses. Princess Margaret especially has a great following among teen-agers and the younger set."

However, it was noted that Margaret was not an extravagant dresser and that a checked dress she first wore during her Italian holiday in 1949 was worn again in 1951. The midnight-blue velvet coat that she wore during the cold winter months, with its fur collar removed, became a new spring coat!

By the end of the year she had moved into the exalted ranks of the World's Best Dressed Women but she did not displace the Duchess of Windsor, who still headed the list put out by the New York Dress Institute. Secretly, Margaret was delighted at just being included.

On November 20 she accompanied her favorite aunt, the Duchess of Kent, on a private visit to Paris which included the British Hertford Hospital Ball.

Margaret was sporting the latest "dangle" earrings with her new wide hair style, and to the cheers of the crowd drove happily off to stay in a suite at the British Embassy that had been occupied at various times by Princess Elizabeth, the Duke of Edinburgh, the Duchess of Kent and Sir Winston Churchill.

With windows that looked out over the chestnut trees to the Avenue Gabriel and beyond the Champs Elysées, her accommodation consisted of a large bedroom with draperies and bedspread of flowered cretonne, a dressing room and a sitting room complete with library, radio and white telephone. The walls were covered with white linen wallpaper decorated with gold stripes. She ate from silver-gilt table plate that formerly had belonged to the Duke of Wellington.

Margaret dined at Maxim's, the restaurant so beloved by her "naughty" great-grandfather, King Edward VII; and then nearly lost her hat when she ascended the Eiffel Tower in a fifty-mile-an-hour wind. Dressed in a fall coat of pale violet with a cloche hat made entirely from peacock feathers, she exclaimed in astonishment, "I never believed Paris was so big before."

On November 24 she had a tea date with a certain General of the Army, Dwight D. Eisenhower, and kept him cooling his heels for twenty minutes at the Supreme Headquarters of the Allied Powers in Europe. He was visibly impatient as he paced up and down in front of his reception hall waiting for the pocket-princess, whose chauffeur gallantly took the blame for her lateness, saying he had taken a wrong turn with the royal car.

However, one look at Margaret and General Ike turned on his own particular brand of smile and good-naturedly said, "Your Royal Highness, it is nice to see you."

"Thank you," laughed Margaret and all was instantly forgiven.

After tea she bid Ike good-by and went night-clubbing until three o'clock in the morning.

At the official dance she waltzed with Paul Auriol, son of President Vincent Auriol, and later flew back to England in a thunderstorm.

Margaret's finances also got a going-over during the year and a little bill to give her a six thousand pounds ($18,000) annuity produced a lively debate in the British House of Commons.

Clement Attlee and Winston Churchill were both involved in it. The Labor Party was in power at the time, and Mr. Attlee, then prime minister, explained that Margaret was left out of the Civil List Act of 1937.

Churchill, who was in a very good humor, said: "The burdens and duties imposed upon the members of the Royal Family become heavier and more exhausting every day. There is no part of the country in which they are not eagerly welcomed to any of the multiplying functions which happily enlighten and relieve our daily life. The effect upon the Royal Family is that of ever increasing toil and duty."

Emrys Hughes, a labor member from Ayrshire, Scotland, caused a ripple of laughter in the House when he asked why fourteen years had passed without the constitutional lawyers' spotting the mistake?

"Can it be that there is a Communist plot, and we have not carefully screened the people who drafted this bill?"

Then he recalled that back in 1937 it was in fact the Labor Party who were against poor Margaret's getting her six thousand pounds, and there were some red faces in the Labor ranks when he noted that Mr. Attlee was one of those who had opposed it at that time.

Not content with this reminder, frugal Scottish laborites added fuel to the flames by staging a one-hour battle to cut the proposed allowance by half. It seemed very ironic to Margaret, the only native-born Scottish princess in the royal family, to know that her own people were squabbling over her allowance.

Finally the issue was settled and Margaret got the full sum that had first been suggested.

Princess Margaret is very careful with her money. She has to be, for she has many calls upon her purse. She is expected to subscribe generously to her favorite charities, she must buy her own clothes (if she were to accept a free pair of nylons somebody would be bound to say she was advertising a certain manufacturer's product) and she always pays for her own transportation. For instance, if she is going by train to Balmoral she pays her own first-class fare and buys any meals she eats en route. When she goes abroad she also provides her own transportation, even if she has been invited. However, if the visit is official and not private, once inside the country of which she is a guest, she takes advantage of the transportation provided by her hosts.

A good example of this was the last visit to the United States of Queen Elizabeth and Prince Philip. They were not given free transportation by the United States until they had actually landed by air in Washington. After that they were official guests of the President and the government.

During the war when nylons were as precious as gold in England, many sympathetic American women sent the two young Princesses nylons as gifts. They were not allowed to accept them and the gifts were passed on to other British girls.

Princess Maragaret does not have to pay to live at Clarence House and the Castle of Mey, for these are her mother's homes. She has not yet set up a house of her own.

In addition to the six thousand pounds a year she gets from the state, Margaret has a private income, part of which she inherited from a friend of the Queen Mother's. Since royal wills are never made public, it is not known what amounts of money were left her by her father or Queen Mary.

Queen Elizabeth, the Queen Mother, and Princess Margaret in the robes which they wore at the coronation of Queen Elizabeth II.

*Queen Mary, Princess Margaret's grandmother, helps to saw wood
during the second World War on her country estate.*

Princess Margaret, just before her 21st birthday.

Princess Margaret, an enthusiastic sportswoman, waits for the beginning of a hunting party.

The royal family attends the theatre in London in 1949.

Princess Margaret and her mother, Queen Elizabeth, leave Buckingham Palace to attend a military review in London.

Princess Margaret presents the winner's cup to her brother-in-law, the Duke of Edinburgh, after a polo match.

The Queen and Princess Margaret attend the Olympic Horse Trials accompanied by Group Captain Peter Townsend in 1953.

Chapter Nine

TRAGEDY

The death of her beloved papa was a most severe shock to Princess Margaret. For three days she did not eat and her sufferings were terrible. In recalling the loss of her father she says, "It seemed as though the whole world were standing still."

She had also lost her other close companion, for with their father's untimely passing Lilibet became Queen of England and a gulf of officialdom came between them.

It was then that friendship, tenderness and a common sympathy for each other drew Margaret and Group-Captain Peter Townsend together. He was at Sandringham when her father died, and for days afterwards was the only one who could raise her even momentarily from the despair into which her grief had cast her.

Through all the stress and strain of a royal funeral, the man behind the scenes, the man who encouraged her at every turn, was Townsend, a man eighteen years her senior. That her father had been fond of the airman was recommendation enough for Princess Margaret. It was only natural that she should turn to him more and more for affection.

King George VI had been in ill-health for some years. On March 12, 1949 he had undergone surgery known as a lumbar sympathectomy to save his right leg from amputation. He was suffering from Buerger's disease, and in his case the wall of the artery conveying the blood to his right leg had narrowed. The operation was outwardly a success, but the King was told that it could result only in a relief for the disease and not a cure. Undaunted, the King gradually returned to his royal duties.

In 1951 he again took sick, this time with influenza which left him with an inflamed spot on his left lung. Subsequent X-ray and bronchoscope examinations revealed he was suffering from a malignant growth on the bronchus of the left lung. On September 23 in the Buhl Room of Buckingham Palace, which had been turned into an operating theater, King George VI underwent what is known as a pneumonectomy—the removal of the left lung. Clement Price Thomas, a prominent chest surgeon, performed the delicate operation. It was found that the King's other lung was already affected and he was suffering from bronchial carcinoma, a quick-spreading kind of lung cancer.

King George knew he had little time left. He was

suffering from two incurable diseases and his life-ex-
pectancy was two years at the most. For his immediate
family the last few months of the King's life were ones
of intense strain. He persisted in doing all the work he
could, although a Council of State was instituted to relieve him of part of it. His wife, Princess Elizabeth,
Princess Margaret, the Duke of Gloucester and the
Princess Royal comprised the Council.

By sheer will-power and persistence he broadcast his
usual Christmas message—though he had to first record
it, due to the paralysis of a vocal chord that followed his
last operation. After the family Christmas party he remained at Sandringham. The King was well enough to
join the local shooting during the crisp, cold January
days, and after gaining eight pounds in weight he returned to London on January 28 with the Queen to bid
farewell to Princess Elizabeth and the Duke of Edinburgh who were setting out for their royal tour of Australia and New Zealand.

Next day George VI left his beloved London for the
last time, and with his wife and younger daughter returned to Sandringham. He was very happy and joked
with everyone about his health, insisting he would show
the doctors and outlive the lot of them. On February 5
he waved the Queen and Princess Margaret good-by and
with his neighbor, Lord Fermoy, set off for a day's
shooting. The King was in fine form, bagging nine hares
and a pigeon. At the day's end, in bidding farewell to
Lord Fermoy and his other shooting companions, he
said: "Well, it's been a very good day's sport, gentlemen.
I will expect you here at nine o'clock on Thursday."

[67]

It had been a good day for everyone. The Queen and Princess Margaret went sailing on the lovely Norfolk Broads and that evening told the King of their day's adventures. Then they all sat around the fireside. On two occasions the King left them briefly—for a look at his golden retriever, Roddy, who was suffering from a thorn in his paw, and for a walk in the gardens.

Then Margaret played for her parents on the piano for an hour, and together the family listened in to the news bulletin to hear what Elizabeth and Philip were doing.

After retiring, the King sat propped up reading in bed. He bade his footman, Daniel Long, good-night.

Next morning the assistant valet, James Macdonald, discovered that his master had died in his sleep. When the first shock was over he informed an officer of the King's household, and a lady in waiting went to waken the Queen. The Queen in turn woke Margaret and told her the news. Her father had died of a coronary thrombosis.

Death in an English home is a very personal thing. Seldom is the body removed to a funeral parlor. It remains in the house with the family; the closed door and the drawn bedroom blinds are a constant reminder of its presence. At Sandringham it was even more personal. The casket was made on the spot from a locally grown oak, and then the King's body was taken to the village church prior to the ceremonial lying-in-state at Westminster Hall in London.

Elizabeth and Philip were flying home from Kenya where, in a tree house, they had first learned the news.

Margaret and her widowed mother, both heavily veiled, followed the casket to the church. The kindly workers on the Sandringham Estate had erected a tarpaulin for them to walk behind so that their grief would not be so readily observed.

In the days that followed, the spotlight fell on the young queen and the high position to which she had so suddenly been called. The new queen was fortunate in one respect—she had Philip to lean on for comfort.

Chapter Ten

LIFE WITH MOTHER

For some months after the death of George VI Princess Margaret and her mother stayed on at Buckingham Palace with the new queen and the Duke of Edinburgh. There was little fear of their treading on each other's toes in the 602-room palace, and time was necessary for the royal change-over of homes. Actually the Queen Mother and Margaret got the better end of the deal, for Clarence House had only recently been renovated and furnished at a cost of some $150,000.

Living in Buckingham Palace has often been compared to camping in a museum, and only at the time of George VI's death was the antiquated central heating system being modernized with new oil burners, and the electrical installations converted to accepted modern standards.

In contrast, Clarence House is pleasant and homey-looking with its outer cream-colored walls, black window frames and doors. It forms part of St. James' Palace, ancient home of Britain's kings and queens. The oldest part dates from 1825-1827 but stands on the site of an earlier Clarence House. George III gave the tenancy to his third eldest son, the Duke of Clarence, later William IV.

The lovable but tragic Princess Charlotte of Wales, daughter of the Prince Regent, is associated with Clarence House. Her royal bridegroom, Prince Leopold, stayed there in 1816 prior to their wedding, and from ten in the morning to five in the afternoon, with the exception of two hours when he drove out in his "plain green chariot," he was cheered by large crowds of Londoners standing in the stable yard. The prince, later in 1831 to be elected King of the Belgians, appeared time and again on the balcony to acknowledge the cheering. While all this was going on, his bride-to-be was spending the morning patiently sitting for her bust by Turnerelli the sculptor.

Later, wearing a gown of silver tinsel with a headdress of diamond roses, Princess Charlotte married Leopold at Carlton House, where her royal grandmother, also named Charlotte, insisted that a Mrs. Campbell, childhood governess to the princess, should ride in the honeymoon carriage with the newlyweds, as she considered it "so improper" they should be alone. The loyal governess stoutly refused to obey the order!

Princess Charlotte later died in childbirth. Witty and beloved of the common people, she had many of Princess Margaret's characteristics and winning ways. She always said what she thought and the people loved it. She was also a girl of great spunk and absolutely refused to obey her father's command to marry William, the unattractive hereditary Prince of Orange. Leopold was the man of her choice and in the end she got her own way. Previously, at a time when she was officially engaged to marry William, the Regent had sent her a list of wedding guests in which she noticed her mother's name was missing. (The Regent refused to acknowledge his wife, Caroline of Brunswick, as queen of England and on his coronation day had the doors of Westminster Abbey locked against her.) Charlotte had promptly scratched out the name of the proposed bridegroom and sent the list back to her father!

The Duke of Clarence brought his bride, Princess Adelaide of Saxe-Coborg-Meiningen, to Clarence House, but complained of the "wretched state of dirt" in his apartments. As a result of this, most of the old house was torn down and remodeled to follow the plans of John Nash, who was also responsible for designing Buckingham Palace. The alterations were completed in 1828 and cost $39,000—a large sum in those days. Clarence House was improved twice after that only to suffer bombing by the Nazis in World War II.

It was almost a wreck when Elizabeth and Philip took over. For years it had been the home of the Duke of Connaught who died in 1942 at the age of ninety-three. It had never been properly wired for electric lighting or completely redecorated for over fifty years. The windows had been blown out by blasts and the gaping holes where they had once been were covered with tar paper. There was only one bathtub in the entire household and the gas system was rusting and falling apart with age.

That was all changed for Elizabeth and Philip, and the former was appalled at the cost. The new central heating system which was installed is among the best in London.

Now the Queen Mother moved in to Clarence House with her valuable collection of modern paintings. Margaret insisted on having her own front door to her small suite which she furnished with pieces of Sheraton furniture. These are all small, for she says, "I am a small person and need small things about me." The bathroom she designed herself has pastel-tinted tiles. The windows look down upon a flower garden.

Most of the rooms at Clarence House are wired for electric power and the Queen Mother had the walls painted in all her favorite light pastel shades and furnished them with choice antiques in traditional taste. The larger rooms have open fireplaces and include two exquisite ormolu and marble chimneypieces by Nash. The kitchens are considered to be among the most up-to-date in Britain. Stainless steel cabinets and equipment line the walls and sinks, and even the tables are of the same material. Most of the cooking apparatus stands in the middle of the room for the greater convenience of the cooks.

Like all Scottish women, the Queen Mother is proud of her domesticity. She likes nothing more than to go into her kitchen and bake scones. Margaret can cook and so can Elizabeth, although Margaret's culinary arts are mainly confined to preparing eggs and bacon for the friends who drop in to visit after the theater.

Clarence House is run on very economical lines and requires only a small staff compared with that considered necessary for a royal home in the past. Some of the employees have been with Margaret and her mother for many years. The old house has come alive again and once more has a fairy princess living within its mellowed walls.

Chapter Eleven

BRITAIN'S QUEEN MUM

The American crowds nicknamed the Queen Mother, "the Queen Mum" when she visited the United States in the fall of 1954. As an American newspaper editorial put it: "You are welcome because you are so nice."

When her father died Margaret said, "I can't leave Mummy now," and the two of them have lived happily together since. Even during the trying days of the Townsend crisis the Queen Mother defied public criticism by allowing her daughter and Townsend to meet at home and discuss their problems together.

"Like mother, like daughter," says the proverb, and it is interesting to take a brief look at the older woman who is Princess Margaret's most frequent companion.

The Queen Mother who told the British nation when her husband died, "My only wish now is that I may

[75]

be allowed to continue the work we sought to do together," is carrying out to the letter the task she has set herself. Londoners have never forgotten that she refused to leave them when, night after night during World War II, the city was a bomb target. They saw her weep openly as she passed through the shattered streets.

A compassionate woman, and one who believes that the Bible should be placed where it can be seen and read in every home, she has learned to give practical help where it is most needed. When one of her long-time maids became an alcoholic, the Queen Mother supported her while she took special treatment in a sanatorium and looked after her for some years afterward until she died.

The Queen Mother is also a firm believer in prayer. When the governor of St. Mary's Hospital in London remarked it was a miracle that the hospital was not hit by bombs during the war, she said, "A miracle? That may be so, but you know, I include St. Mary's in my prayers every night!"

Nonsectarian in many of her beliefs, she never misses a Sunday morning service or early communion. She heard the American evangelist Billy Graham preach a command sermon before her daughter, Queen Elizabeth II.

Like many Britons, the Queen Mother is fascinated by murder cases, and often on a free afternoon she slips quietly away from Clarence House and listens to gory details related to her by the country's foremost criminologists and poison analysts. She also likes to see the evidence in the police laboratory collections and perches on a high stool to do so.

Now in her late fifties, the Queen Mother is still youthful in appearance. Her hair is still unstreaked with gray, although it has somewhat darkened in a way that is characteristic of Scottish folk. Her complexion is flawless; she uses little make-up and only a light lipstick. Her energy still seems boundless. During an informal evening spent with young friends in New York City, she wore everybody out with her enthusiasm, sang popular songs with Yale students, and later bemoaned the fact that she had "to go home to bed." Next morning she was up with the lark to fulfill a host of public engagements.

Since becoming the Queen Mother she has given herself the freedom of dressing as she likes rather than in the manner she thinks a Queen should look. Unkind people used to say she could never leave anything at home; that on most occasions she was overburdened with furs and jewels. Nowadays the Queen Mother has forsaken her frills and feathers and wears simpler clothes that really do her justice.

She is still one of the least photogenic of all public figures. A cameraman once remarked, "That little woman has grounds for a libel suit every time she is photographed."

She is quite aware of her middle age and is probably the only celebrity living to send her new portrait back to a prominent photographer with instructions to put back the lines and make her look a little older! "I have battled my way through a number of years," she said, "and cannot have come through completely unscathed."

She loves her grandchildren, Prince Charles and Princess Anne, and like many another grandmother, spoils them. Queen Elizabeth II consults her mother daily on various royal problems. The Queen Mother is on particularly good terms with Prince Philip, her son-in-law.

She never has received the Duchess of Windsor, although the Duchess is the woman indirectly responsible for making her a queen. However, she does occasionally have the Duke of Windsor in for a cup of tea when he is visiting London on his own.

In spite of being able to make others feel happy and at ease when in her company, the Queen Mother has few really intimate friends. The two women nearest her, aside from close relatives, have died—Mrs. Ronald Grenville at whose home in Surrey she spent her honeymoon and who left Princess Margaret a great deal of money; and Lady Helen Graham, her first lady in waiting.

She is particularly devoted to her family and when her niece, Viscountess Anson, eldest daughter of the late Honorable John Bowes-Lyon, a divorcee, married Prince Georg of Denmark, Acting Military Attaché of the Danish Embassy, September 18, 1950, she attended the reception, following the wedding at Glamis Castle, with Princess Margaret. Although the ceremony was not performed by a Church of England priest but by a minister of another denomination, the Queen Mother did not escape some criticism for being present at the wedding reception of a divorced person.

Unlike her elder daughter, the Queen Mother when

she is not off on some official function has little regard for time. She sleeps late, breakfasts at nine in her room or with Princess Margaret, and then leisurely settles down to read the morning papers.

She keeps up with all news items about the royal family though she doesn't take the trouble of writing, as she used to do, to editors responsible for printing stories and photographs she doesn't like. She still receives a great deal of mail from people she doesn't know, and is very careful to answer it. Luckily she is able to cope with her mail very quickly and, although she isn't required to write or even sign the letters herself, dictates them or tells her ladies in waiting what they are to say.

The Queen Mother, like Margaret, can also be unpredictable when she likes and is certainly no stuffed shirt. She proved this during her last visit to the United States when it was announced she would not reply if spoken to by reporters or people in the crowd. One newspaperwoman thought she would find out if this was true, and as the Queen Mother was leaving an official function said, "Good-by, Your Majesty."

The Queen Mother turned, smiled sweetly and replied, "Good-by."

Exactly the same thing happened when she visited St. Martin's Protestant Episcopal Church in Harlem, New York City, where most of the congregation are of British West Indian heritage. She was scheduled to step briefly out of her car, accept a bouquet and then drive immediately to the Cathedral of St. John the Divine. The Queen Mother did step out of her car and stayed for several minutes when the Sunday School children began to sing "God Save the Queen." Leaving her attendants, she walked into the crowd, shaking hands, talking, and even allowing a little blind girl to feel her hands.

Margaret's mother is quite resigned to her plumpness and was actually pleased when a Canadian girl wrote to the newspapers complaining when the Queen Mother had been forced to diet and lose fourteen pounds to look streamlined for the Canadian tour of 1939. The girl said, "It's not nice. We want to think of our Queen as a mother and none of us would like to hear that our mothers were losing weight."

The Queen Mother has a good appetite and, with the exception of white bread and potatoes, eats exactly what she likes. Her pink-and-white complexion is still unblemished by the years. She drinks very little, sometimes taking a glass of claret or a cocktail. Seldom does she smoke and never in public.

Like her elder daughter, Queen Elizabeth, she has never been one to exert herself in strenuous sports. She likes walking her dogs, especially when they can roam for miles together on the lonely Scottish moors. In London she exercises her dogs herself, as Margaret does, for she doesn't trust anybody else to do it for her. Although she can drive a car, she hasn't done so for the last twenty years. She has a great fear of speed, and can at times be accused of being a back-seat driver!

A lover of horse racing, she owns horses which race under her special colors—a blue and buff tunic, black cap and gold tassel. The Queen Mother pays her own stable expenses. She is not alone in her love for the turf; Queen Elizabeth II, whose annual racing bill amounts to

$60,000 a year, is another enthusiast. To the latter the year 1954 was especially outstanding, for she topped the entire list of winners in the flat-racing season. No reigning monarch had done such a thing before and she took more prize money, $120,000, than all the other owners. Her best horse was Aureole, winner of the King George VI and Queen Elizabeth Stakes at Ascot.

The Queen Mother is still entitled to sign herself Elizabeth Regina. She receives an allowance of $210,000 a year, and since the death of George VI has purchased the ancient Castle of Mey in Scotland as a country home for herself and Margaret, restoring it at an estimated cost of $30,000. Central heating has been installed and a new roof added. One of the large carpets was presented her by a group of convicts!

Chapter Twelve

RING THE BELLS

Queen Elizabeth II was marching down the corridor of Buckingham Palace when she came upon a tradeswoman waiting patiently outside a particular door.

"Didn't you have an appointment for half an hour ago?" asked the puzzled Elizabeth.

"Yes, ma'am," answered the other woman, "but it's quite all right."

Elizabeth frowned and, opening the door, went in search of her sister. Almost immediately Margaret appeared and apologized profusely. Elizabeth still likes to tell Margaret what to do.

In spite of their difference in rank, Elizabeth's being queen made little change in her attitude toward Margaret. She still tried to mother her and particularly resented many of the stories concerning the "gay Princess Margaret and her countless beaux."

Margaret took longer than any of them to recover from the shock of George VI's death. She still had long spells of melancholy and weeping, and sometimes they could hardly get her to eat. Breakfast often consisted only of coffee and orange juice, and it was at times necessary for her to take sedatives to induce sleep. Then, too, Margaret remembered other princesses who were fated to become the "forgotten royal sisters" of history. However, in her own way she was still devoted to Elizabeth and, with the help of Philip, succeeded in improving the young queen's tastes in fashion. Up to then Elizabeth had copied her mother, and often the result was clothes that were too old for her. She had always worn pastel shades because, she said, "Mummie likes them." Under her sister's and Philip's guidance Queen Elizabeth emerged in bright, colorful clothes cut in simple lines that did her full justice.

Margaret would get very annoyed at photographs that did not flatter her sister. Once while examining a family photograph album she exclaimed in annoyance, "Oh, why do all these pictures make Lilibet look like a stuffed pig?"

On May 23, 1952, Princess Margaret and her widowed mother made history when they became the first British royal women to fly in a jet airliner. No queen or princess had ever flown so fast or so high before. They took off on a 1,850-mile sightseeing trip over a large part of Western Europe in a new British Comet. En route they flew over France, Switzerland and Italy before returning across Southern France to England.

At forty-thousand feet they enjoyed a picnic lunch and at one time traveled at a speed of five hundred miles an hour. They had selected their own route which gave them a birds-eye view of the Swiss Alps from a height of seven miles. Both the Queen Mother and Margaret took turns at sitting beside the pilot in the cockpit and when it was over said they had thoroughly enjoyed the trip.

On July 8, Margaret was off to Norfolk to open the new orthopedic unit at Norfolk and Norwich Hospital where she showed great interest in the apparatus and insisted upon having her hand X-rayed.

She was then to have visited the Jenny Lind Hospital for Children, Norwich, and to tour the wards, but was stopped by the authorities because of a suspected case of infantile paralysis. The Princess immediately thought of all the disappointed children there would be that day, and she directed her chauffeur to drive her car slowly through the hospital grounds so that they should at least see her from the windows.

Her next public engagement was on July 18 when she journeyed to much-blitzed Plymouth to open the Naafi Club, the latest building to be finished in the reconstruction of the blitzed city. The new club cost $1,200,000, and Margaret thoroughly inspected the restaurant, kitchens and walnut-paneled tavern, together with the residential wing built to accommodate members of the women's services and service families. Later she opened the new ballroom but didn't stop to try it out.

For the first time since her father's death, on July 26 she took time off to visit the theater. The play was Shakespeare's *Much Ado About Nothing*.

When she returned to Balmoral, Scotland, for yet another birthday, this time her twenty-second, once more all the gossips were asking, "Will she or won't she announce her engagement?" though nobody seemed to know for sure from which of her several boy friends she was willing to accept a ring. Once more Margaret disappointed the British—who love nothing better than a romance—to say nothing of the Americans, who like it even more.

A florist at Aberdeen received an order for a birthday bouquet to be sent to Margaret from an unknown admirer in Danville, Illinois. The order specified it must contain twenty-two white gladioli and twenty-two white roses—but the florist was not allowed to disclose either the message or pseudonym of the sender. Princess Margaret was just as puzzled as those who read of her "mystery admirer" and doesn't know to this day if it was male or female.

The morning was dry and cloudy on Upper Deeside but the sun broke through in time for the birthday lunch held on the open moor at Gairnshiel. Once more Margaret was toasted in champagne—but this year for the first time her beloved Papa was missing and Philip, who had been out all morning grouse shooting, proposed the toast in his stead. Margaret received more messages of congratulatons than ever. This was one princess the world had determined should never be forgotten.

On October 16, wearing a dress of white tulle, she arrived at the Odeon Cinema, Leicester Square, London, for the premiere performance of Charlie Chaplir's *Lime-light* and was cheered by a crowd of four thousand. Chaplin and his wife, together with two of their children, were presented to the smiling Princess before the performance.

On the thirtieth of the month she arrived to attend a performance of the all-American show *Porgy and Bess* wearing a hip-length ermine jacket over a long, black taffeta gown. The show, which was playing to capacity houses in London, pleased her and she expressed especial delight at Cab Galloway's portrayal of Sportin' Life.

She launched the T.E.V. *Maori* at Newcastle-Upon-Tyne on November 27—a twin-screw turbo-electric passenger vessel of eighth thousand gross tons ordered by the Union Steamship Company of New Zealand. It was again a day of memories, for the last time a member of the royal family had performed a launching ceremony at that particular shipyard was on February 21, 1939, when her father had launched the battleship H.M.S. *King George V*.

On December 8 she went to the theater again—this time to see the Crazy Gang star in *Ring the Bells* at the Victoria Palace, and when a bottle of champagne was tossed into the audience Princess Margaret reached up and caught it.

A note appeared in the American press which read: "A good-looking brunette sitting in the sixth row of the orchestra made the catch and was all smiles."

Chapter Thirteen

SADNESS AND A CORONATION

The year 1953 was also Coronation Year, and nobody was looking forward more to the crowning of her grand-daughter than Britain's beloved Queen Mary. She resented the fact that she was growing old, and so did her late husband's subjects. There were many sighs when she used a wheel chair while visiting an exhibition. She was unable to attend the funeral of her son, George VI, and stood quietly at a window of Marlborough House as his funeral cortege passed.

The two small princesses, Elizabeth and Margaret, had been her special joy and she was determined to live to see Elizabeth's coronation day, but fate willed otherwise. On March 2 the aged queen had a recurrence of gastric trouble. She would have been eighty-six years old

[87]

in May. Her family hurried to her bedside; the Duke of Windsor arrived from America. Margaret came with Elizabeth and Philip to say a last good-by at four forty-six on the afternoon of March 24.

Late that night while an anxious crowd waited outside Marlborough House a bulletin was posted which read: "While sleeping peacefully, Queen Mary died at twenty minutes past ten o'clock." It was signed by Sir Horace Evans and Lord Webb-Johnson. So ended the life of a great personality.

One of the most endearing tributes to her memory came from the Reverend L. M. Charles-Edwards, vicar of St. Martin's-in-the-Fields, of whose church Queen Mary was a parishioner. "As she grew older," he said, "she found it increasingly difficult to climb the rather steep stairs leading to the royal box where she always sat. It was suggested that she might prefer a seat at the front of the church, but she preferred to make the effort to climb the stairs, because, she said, 'When I come to St. Martin's Church I come to worship the Almighty and not to be stared at.' "

The same vicar remembered that once when he asked for toys, particularly a rocking horse, to be placed in a part of the church where children could play while their young parents worshipped, Queen Mary sent a message next day regretting she had no rocking horse to give him but offering other toys.

There was nothing ostentatious about her funeral. A family service was held in the private chapel at Marlborough House the Sunday before, followed by a lying-in-state at Westminster Hall where her fellow Londoners could come and say good-by. She was buried by her husband's side in St. George's Chapel, Windsor. It was a sunny spring day; birds were singing; there was no military pomp, drums beating or elaborate trappings. The Queen Mother, with her daughters Elizabeth II and Margaret, slipped quietly into their places just before the service began. Queen Mary's favorite hymns, "Abide With Me" and "Glorious Things Of Thee Are Spoken," were sung, and then after Elizabeth had scattered earth from a silver bowl on her grandmother's casket, Grannie England was laid to rest.

The official period of mourning for Queen Mary was greatly shortened in view of the impending coronation of Elizabeth on June 2. Although Princess Margaret had been unable to attend the wedding of Princess Josephine Charlotte of Belgium and Prince Jean of Luxembourg because of the court mourning for her grandmother, she continued to fill her long list of engagements.

In April she opened Rowlinson Secondary Technical School, Norton, Sheffield, where she delivered one of her best speeches to date. "In this mechanical age," she said "we must not forget that we are, before anything else, human beings, and not cogs in a vast machine. It is not enough that education should aim at making men and women good technicians."

Although she does not always do the actual writing of her speeches, Princess Margaret makes a point of dictating the general outline of what she wants to say. Later she goes carefully through the finished speech, and if it contains anything she doesn't care for, out comes her blue pencil. Like Grannie England, she doesn't like wishy-washy speeches that have been written just to please the audiences. Margaret prefers to speak the truth even if it doesn't always please. Neither does she like to be asked to give a speech she considers too long.

As with the Queen Mother, her spontaneous comments and remarks are the most pleasing. When she visited an orphanage in Crowborough, Sussex, a small child asked if she could play a guitar. Margaret said, "I'll try," and put down her bouquet and strummed a few notes to the delight of her young audience.

However, in her speeches she has never been quite so outspoken as Philip, her brother-in-law. Since he is a man, she probably feels he can get away with it. She was more upset than any other member of the royal family when Lord Altringham and some others criticized her beloved Elizabeth's speeches. To Margaret it seemed all the more despicable as Elizabeth, because of her position as queen, couldn't answer back. One can only happily surmise how these critics would have fared if the sharp-witted Margaret had been left alone with them for a few minutes.

After her speech at Sheffield she went to Rotherham, twelve miles away, where she attended a service to commemorate the fiftieth anniversary of the attainment by the town of county borough status. The north door of the parish church that had been sealed for more than a century was opened for the Princess to walk through.

In the light of subsequent events, it was a little ironic that Princess Margaret should be chosen to represent the Queen and fly to Norway for the wedding of Princess Ragnhild, granddaughter of King Haakon, to a commoner, Erling Lorentzen. On March 14 she flew to Oslo, and was welcomed at Fornebu Airfield by the King of Norway; members of the Norwegian royal family; Sir Michael Wright, the British Ambassador; and members of the British colony in that country. Thousands of people gathered on both sides of the highway leading from the airfield to the royal palace and cheered the British princess.

Margaret, in a black skirt, white jacket and black velvet beret, looked even smaller than she really is, standing beside the tall Norwegian monarch. The fairytale wedding was held in the parish church of Asker, near the Crown Prince's country home at Skaugum. It was spring in Norway and the fruit trees on the mountainsides were white with blossoms.

A canopy draped with red, white and blue cloth had been built outside the church, and an archway garlanded with lilies-of-the-valley and rosebuds stretched across the roadway, with a plaque on it bearing the initials of the bride and bridegroom, R and E. After the wedding the bride, to be known in future as Princess Ragnhild Mrs. Lorentzen, and her groom drove in an open landau to the town of Asker and then back to the Crown Prince's home for the wedding breakfast.

On May 17, Margaret made an appearance on the palace balcony with King Haakon and Crown Prince Olav to inspect twenty thousand children from Oslo's fifty-three schools as they marched past in traditional fashion to celebrate Norwegian National Festival Day.

She also found time to visit the Kon-Tiki Museum which houses the balsa-wood raft on which six men drifted across the Pacific Ocean in the summer of 1947. Thor Heyerdahl, leader of the expedition, explained all the details of the raft which had traveled 4,300 miles in 101 days.

Margaret returned to London in a Viscount turbo-jet aircraft where two thousand Britishers were waiting to greet her.

On May 20, she attended the Red, White and Blue Ball at London's fashionable Dorchester Hotel and was surrounded by eight of her beaux, the Earl of Dalkeith, Viscount Hambleden, Billy Wallace, Tom Egerton, David Naylor-Leyland, Lord Patrick Plunket and Prince Nicholas of Yugoslavia.

Bubbling over with delight, she arrived promptly at eleven in the evening, wearing a tulip-style gown of pale blue satin and collar of diamonds. Partnered by Lord Hambleden, she opened the ball with a fox trot. The room was lighted with a thousand candles, and for decorative purposes sixteen suits of armor in their mailed fists held balloons instead of battle-axes. Margaret seemed delighted with so much male attention and later told Prince Nicholas and Billy Wallace with whom she was sitting out a samba, "It is great fun to meet my old friends again. I must come dancing more often."

Together they enjoyed the gala midnight cabaret at which Eddie Fisher was the chief attraction. Margaret, who was determined to meet the American entertainer, afterward invited him to sit with her at the top table. She did most of the talking, plying Fisher with loads of questions about his singing while with pursed lips he listened patiently.

At Margaret's request Eddie later sang "Outside of Heaven" and the Princess led the other guests in singing the refrain. At two o'clock she used the royal prerogative and asked for an extension of the ball, and Mark Bonham-Carter claimed her in a waltz that lasted exactly fifteen minutes. At two-thirty she reluctantly said good night and left for home.

On June 2 Margaret drove in state with the Queen Mother to Westminster Abbey for the coronation of her beloved Lilibet. Looking every inch a princess, she walked in procession through the abbey to a special seat of honor.

Her gown was one of the most beautiful seen that day; like the Queen's and the Queen Mother's, it was designed by Norman Hartnell. Of white satin with tightly fitting bodice, square neckline and short petal-edged sleeves, it was described by a columnist as looking "as if it had caught the shining of moonlight and dewdrops." The medallions of *broderie anglais* were embroidered with silver, diamante and pearls. From a tracery of silver thread hung pendant pear-shaped pearls which were also used to fringe the gown's hem and short sleeves.

Margaret's state robes were of ermine, purple and gold. She wore a small gold coronet and her whole appearance was one of a story-book princess. It was Elizabeth's coronation, and the new Queen looked very beautiful, but for a few brief moments as the petite Margaret walked slowly through the Abbey, she completely stole the show.

As a child Margaret had always loved dressing up, and she liked to see Elizabeth dress up. She was more excited than her sister when, as children, Elizabeth was attired in all her finery to be bridesmaid to Princess Marina of Greece, later the Duchess of Kent.

During the long pageantry of the coronation service, Margaret's eyes never left her elder sister's face. She carefully followed all the prayers and repeated the responses with deep devotion, and when her beloved Lilibet was crowned, the "little sister" wept.

What were the emotions of the Queen Mother and Princess Margaret that morning in the solemn atmosphere of Westminster Abbey?

For the Queen Mother it must have been the climax in a chain of events that had lifted her from the obscurity of a lonely Scottish castle to her own crowning as consort of King George VI. Now their eldest child, a daughter of both England and Scotland, was being crowned in her own right.

As the organ music filled the fine old church perhaps her thoughts strayed to Grannie England and to her father-in-law, George V, who had always treated her like his own daughter. Above all she may have thought of her quiet devoted husband whose lifework she had vowed to carry on.

For Princess Margaret there were probably thoughts of a happy childhood; of the wonderful years of growing up she had shared with the patient, devoted Elizabeth. Would things be so very different now that Elizabeth was really crowned? Would her ever-growing duties as sovereign widen the inevitable gulf between them?

Elizabeth, she knew, had accepted her destiny with quiet resignation as their father had done—and there on that early June day Margaret did the same.

Chapter Fourteen

RUMORS OF A ROMANCE

When the first changes to the Regency Act were suggested in order that the Queen's husband, the Duke of Edinburgh, might replace Princess Margaret as regent in case of her sister's death, there was immediate speculation that the reasons might lie in the reports that Margaret wished to marry Royal Air Force Group-Captain Peter Townsend.

Sir Winston Churchill, then prime minister, announced July 21 that his government planned to introduce in the House of Commons legislature relieving Princess Margaret of the responsibilities of acting as regent in the event of Elizabeth's death. In New Zealand, Prime Minister Keith Holyoake confirmed reports that the Commonwealth prime ministers had agreed to the changes.

Before the Regency Act was amended it had stated that in the event of the death or incapacity of Queen Elizabeth before her son Prince Charles was eighteen, Princess Margaret, would become regent (acting sovereign) as the adult next in succession to the throne. Even before the accession of Elizabeth, the Court and Cabinet discussed an amendment to the act to designate the Queen's husband, Prince Philip, as regent. At the time of the coronation, the commonwealth prime ministers gave their approval to such a change.

The Regency Act was amended in 1953 and now reads: "An act to provide that, in the event of a Regency becoming necessary under the Regency Act, 1937, His Royal Highness the Duke of Edinburgh shall in certain circumstances be the Regent, to provide that the heir apparent or heir presumptive to the Throne shall be deemed for the purposes of that Act to be of full age if he or she has attained the age of eighteen years. . . ."

This all boils down to the fact that now should Queen Elizabeth die or lose her senses, Philip would be regent until his son Charles is eighteen. He would therefore have the duty of training his own son. Prior to the change in 1953, Margaret, as next adult in line of accession to the throne, would have become regent and responsible for bringing up Charles. There were people who saw in these proposed changes to the act implications that the Princess wished to be free of them in order to marry Townsend.

What of Townsend himself?

Nobody could deny he was a brave man. His World War II record as a fighter pilot during the Battle of

Britain was proof of that. One of "the few," he was shot down in Kent, England, and treated in the little cottage-hospital at Hawkhurst for a badly injured foot.

Good-looking in the gaunt English movie star tradition, he wears his wavy hair longer than would please the average American male. Now past forty, he has weathered the years well and still looks much younger than he actually is.

Peter Townsend is the sort of man who forgives his enemies. During the Battle of Britain he shot a Heinkel down over Whitby, Yorkshire. As he watched it fall to destruction he made a promise to try and see any of its crew who might survive. Next day with two of his own men he visited Karl Missy in Whitby Memorial Hospital. Karl's leg had ben shot off by Townsend's guns.

Karl remembers Peter Townsend.

"This man who shot me down was my first visitor," he says, "and I shall never forget him. He was so full of life and gaiety and warmth of feeling. First he patted me on the shoulder. Then he produced a bag of oranges and bananas from behind his back; and two packets of cigarettes.

"He sat at my bedside and we tried to talk. It was difficult. I knew only a few words of English and he very little German. But we managed. We tried to talk about our jobs in the air. When language failed, he straddled his chair to imitate an aeroplane seat and made signs. Before leaving my bedside, Townsend said, 'You're a good boy. Get better soon.' "

Karl Missy, now a master plumber, and Peter Townsend had a reunion in 1955 at Düsseldorf where the latter was riding in a horse show.

During the war years Townsend had a red felt heart embroidered on white cotton with his name—and stitched into a sliced muffin! It was his mascot made for him by actress Gwen Ffrangcon-Davies who was then appearing with John Gielgud and Jack Hawkins in *The Importance of Being Earnest*. It was Gielgud's idea to give the muffins to the R.A.F., boys as mementoes.

Townsend had a reputation among his men for being even-tempered and patient. "It just comes from inside him," one recalls.

Another wrote of him in 1940, "I bet he'll do the best of all of us in this war."

Born in Rangoon, Burma, Peter Townsend is the son of a British army officer and was brought up to be a gentleman. When the late King George VI picked equerries of honor from among young officers to serve for three-year terms in Buckingham Palace, Peter Townsend was one of them.

The ailing King took a keen liking to the young fighter ace who could talk on any subject, were it horses, dogfights with the enemy or pheasant shooting. Townsend also charmed the King's wife with his good manners and courtesies. Princess Elizabeth was friendly, and Margaret, then in the gawky schoolgirl stage, adored him, simply because he chose to treat her as a grown-up and not just as the "darling of the family." Besides, they had something in common; they were witty. And if the other members of the royal household didn't always appreciate her jokes, Peter did—and quite often matched them with his own.

Although Townsend had warned the R.A.F. boys serving under his command that marriages made in time of war made widows, he himself fell in love with the prettiest of three sisters, beautiful Rosemary Pawle. They were married just six weeks later in the Parish Church of Much Hadham.

Two sons, Giles and Hugo George, were born to them. The younger boy was named in honor of the King. Like many other wartime romances, the marriage was doomed to failure and Townsend divorced his wife on the grounds of adultery. He retained custody of both children. Mrs. Townsend felt that their break-up occurred because of the long periods of separation when her husband's life was completely filled with his duties at the palace.

Margaret, heartbroken after the death of her father, had turned to Townsend for comfort. He appeared as a tower of strength to her at a time when her personal grief was forgotten by others. At that time interest was centered on her elder sister, the new queen. Riding with the handsome air ace in Windsor Park or attending the races with him, Margaret found a wonderful and understanding friend. That he was then thirty-eight—almost old enough to be her father—made little difference in her feeling toward him.

Townsend had risen in office to be Deputy Master of the Royal Household and later Comptroller. In 1947 he had been sent to South Africa to arrange formal protocol for the royal family's tour. On that occasion Princess Elizabeth was "love-sick and miserable" for she was undergoing a "test" period of separation from Prince Philip with whom she was in love.

Unlike the days of the Edward VIII-Wallis Simpson

affair, British newspapers began to publish whispers and rumors of Margaret's supposed romance. In Edward's case, American newspapers had arrived in England with passages reporting his love for a twice-divorced woman conveniently snipped out.

The rumors concerning Margaret and Peter were not new; they had been in the air for a year. They first came to a head in July when a few newspapers mentioned the gossip.

On June 14, *The People,* a large London Sunday paper, said: "The story is, of course, utterly untrue," and called on the authorities to deny and so "stop the scandalous rumors."

By July 2 the fat was really in the fire. Townsend, thrice-decorated Battle of Britain hero, after nine years of perfect service, was suddenly leaving the royal court for the obscure post of air attaché in Brussels.

Embarrassing questions were asked in Parliament and all of England was talking. Laborite Emrys Hughes asked, "Is there any really good reason why there should be a new air attaché appointed in Brussels?"

He was told by Minister of State, Selwyn Lloyd, "There is an air attaché at Brussels. He is being replaced at the present time, and in the view of Her Majesty's Government it is necessary to have such an officer in that post."

Then Marcus Lipton, another Labor member of parliament, demanded assurances that the British Cabinet had not interfered with Princess Margaret's personal life. Most emphatically he was told by Chancellor of the

Exchequer, Richard A. Butler, that such a matter had never been brought before Her Majesty's advisers.

The British press was accused of violating the "canon of good manners" by the weekly *Church of England Newspaper*. A leading Roman Catholic publication, the *Catholic Herald* openly opposed the rumored match saying that Princess Margaret should be made to surrender all royal rank and status should she marry the divorced Captain Townsend.

Then the staid London *Times* came out with its most searching comment on royal affairs since the abdication crisis of 1936. "Based on the flimsiest structure of supposition, it has been given unforgivably the shape of scandal," part of the editorial said. The *Times* opposition to Edward VIII's marriage was believed generally to be a big factor in his renouncing the throne.

At the same time the *Tribune,* a Left-wing Labor weekly published an article asserting that Queen Elizabeth II had already sought advice from the Cabinet as to whether her sister could marry the airman. The *Tribune* said the Cabinet's answer was, No.

People in all walks of life took sides on the issue of Margaret's romance—even the clergy.

The Reverend T. F. Charlton, rector of Dallington in Sussex, thought fit to write in his parish magazine: "I feel I must say something, publicly, about the persecution (for it can hardly be called less) to which Princess Margaret has been subjected recently in certain sections of the press.

"The interest displayed in the Princess's private affairs,

based on who knows what of backstage tittle-tattle, can only be described as disgusting, and all hearsay. The distress it must have caused the Queen and Queen Mother can be well imagined."

Even the then Archbishop of York, the late Dr. Cyril Garbett, a charming and outspoken man, had recently made a strong plea for more charity on the part of the Church of England in its attitude toward divorce.

Adultery, he said, should never be regarded as "the one unforgivable sin," and on the question of degree of innocence or guilt he declared, "Many who have gone through the divorce courts have a right to our sympathy and not our blame."

On July 16 the London *Daily Mirror,* a tabloid with a circulation of four and a half million readers, printed the result of a readers' poll on Margaret's right to marry Townsend. The response was startling: 67,907 readers said Yes, and only 2,235 No.

Meantime, Peter Townsend began what was called his "exile" in Brussels, and Margaret, along with other members of her family, carried on her daily tasks as if nothing had happened.

In the midst of all the gossip and speculation that followed she flew with her mother to Southern Rhodesia for the Rhodes Centenary celebrations.

Questioned in Italy as to whether Princess Margaret was really in love with the handsome air ace, her "wicked uncle," the Duke of Windsor, replied with a sphinx-like smile, "Ask her."

Chapter Fifteen

A SPARKLING VALENTINE

Only forty-seven years ago King George V's sister was left by the death of her father in circumstances very similar to those of Princess Margaret. However, whereas Princess Victoria had no public life apart from her mother, later living in seclusion at Iver, Princess Margaret has become an integral part of the British crown.

During Princess Margaret's 1955 tour of the Caribbean she carried out nearly one hundred official engagements on her own. Beforehand, she expressed a wish to mix as freely as possible during her visit with the inhabitants of the British West Indies. There are no more loyal people in the British Empire than the West Indians. Many of those who have emigrated to the

United States religiously cling to their British citizenship. They are extremely fond of British royalty.

Although by constitutional tradition the royal family takes no part in politics, the Princess's visit was firmly approved by the British Colonial Office. It was acknowledged that the visit of the Queen's sister would boost British prestige and strengthen ties betwen the scattered islanders and Whitehall.

For many years the economic distress of the West Indies had been a source of self-reproach to the British Government, but until five or six years before Princess Margaret's visit little had been done to remedy it. During her Caribbean tour the Princess knew she would come across many problems of vital significance to the inhabitants; poverty, poor housing conditions, racial tension and economic underdevelopment. Although she would not be able to make a long and serious study of these problems, throughout her visit she would be thrown up against them.

Hundreds of Jamaicans who had emigrated since World War II from their native islands to Britain's large cities, in search of work and prosperity, eagerly awaited reports of Margaret's visit to their homeland.

For weeks she had been making preparations to leave, and although the bulk of her gay summer wardrobe had been sent ahead on the royal yacht *Britannia,* which would later transport her from island to island, there were still last-minute fittings for other dresses that would go with her on the plane.

Norman Hartnell supplied the evening gowns for

which he is famous and Victor Stiebel, another exclusive designer, the pretty evening dresses and suits the Princess wears to such advantage. Simone Mirman, a French milliner now established in London, designed her hats. Several new color arrangements were created especially for the West Indian wardrobe and were given such enticing names as Caribbean Gold, Bermuda Blue and Sugar Cane.

A pathway of tulips and daffodils led from the royal lounge at the airport to the B.O.A.C. stratocruiser *Canopus* in which the Princess flew to Trinidad, the first port of call. Her sister, Prince Philip and the Queen Mother accompanied an excited Margaret to the plane to see her off. For Margaret her pending trip was the fulfillment of a lifelong ambition to visit the Western Hemisphere.

The Princess, who had first stopped to say good-by to Prince Charles and Princess Anne, was warmly dressed in a close-fitting coat of sea green with a tiny feathered hat to match. She stood alone on the steps of the plane, a tiny figure in the gray mid-winter light, waving to the crowd and blowing kisses to her relatives.

The *Canopus* was newly decorated in blue, gray and white for the trip. The two-decker aircraft had been converted for such trips for the Queen and Prince Philip when sleeping berths and dressing rooms were provided. On the lower deck there was a cocktail bar and, as the stratocruiser's normal passenger complement was sixty, there was ample room for the twelve people accompanying Margaret on her flight. A crew of twelve, including a stewardess, were commanded by Captain Peter Fair, a veteran B.O.A.C. flyer and former R.A.F. officer who already had made the Atlantic crossing four hundred times. Air-conditioning and pressurization were such that the *Canopus* could be kept comfortable at heights up to thirty thousand feet during its long flight. Its cruising speed was 325 miles per hour and an air escort provided by the Royal Air Force accompanied it.

The Princess was attended by two ladies in waiting, both girls of more or less her own age. Iris Peake, daughter of the Right Honorable Osbert Peake, Minister of Pensions and National Insurance, and of Lady Joan Peake, daughter of the seventh Earl of Essex, served as official lady in waiting. She had worked in the British Foreign Office during World War II and afterwards was employed for some years in the research department of the Conservative Central Office. She acted as Princess Margaret's maid of honor at the coronation of Elizabeth II and in 1953 accompanied the Princess on the tour of Southern Rhodesia.

The extra lady in waiting was Lady Elizabeth Cavendish, a childhood friend of the Queen and Princess Margaret, and a frequent guest at their house parties. In her twenties, she is the elder of the two sisters of the eleventh Duke of Devonshire and was once a social welfare worker among the poor of London's East End.

Before leaving Britain's shores, Princess Margaret received a telegram of *bon voyage* from the Lord Mayor on behalf of the people of London. The Afro West Indian Society and Culture Club representing West Indian immigrants in Britain expressed the fond hope that Margaret would "seek out the true way of life in the West Indies and know the grave problems the people face."

The Press Secretary to the Queen replied to misleading reports concerning the Princess's itinerary:

"The programme has been planned on the principle that the Princess Margaret will make at least one speech in each territory to be visited. Her Royal Highness will also reply to addresses of welcome and speak at other selected ceremonies.

"Her Royal Highness will, of course, shake hands with all of the considerable number of persons who are introduced to her.

"In the early planning Her Royal Highness expressed the wish that arrangements should be made for her to mingle with the guests at the various gatherings, and wherever practicable this has been planned.

"On short drives Her Royal Highness will often use an open car if weather conditions permit. At rallies, in order to give the children and other spectators the best chance of seeing the Princess, a standard jeep or Land Rover will be provided by the local authorities. All the vehicles to be used are being provided from local resources."

The royal plane encountered strong head winds over the Atlantic, and instead of landing as arranged at Gander, Newfoundland, the pilot diverted his course to Dorval Airport, Montreal. A crowd of two hundred Canadians gathered near the plane in two-below-zero cold but were told the Princess was sleeping and would not make an appearance.

Another brief stop was at Montego Bay airport,

Jamaica, on the morning of February 1. Brilliant sunshine greeted the Princess who was met by Governor and Lady Foot. The Princess stayed for an hour and a half, gladly accepting the governor's suggestion for a drive through the countryside.

From the moment Princess Margaret arrived at Piarco Airport, Port-of-Spain, Trinidad, she had the Caribbean at her feet. During both a stirring and affectionate welcome she was called a "lovely fairy." From the pen of a local poet came the greeting: "Hail Princess Margaret, gorgeous, dainty flower, wafting rare fragrance from your regal bower across the heavenly canopy of blue, with boundless loyalty we welcome you."

The Princess was visibly touched. Nothing in her life had been quite like this and she entered fully into the spirit of her visit. She gave of herself to the people and they reciprocated.

The guard of honor, waiting to welcome her ashore, were resplendent in gleaming helmets, white blouses and black trousers. At Arima Race Course there were loyal greetings from the mayor and songs sung by hundreds of excited schoolchildren. There's no holding back West Indians when they want to sing, and in Margaret they found a ready listener.

Back through the crowded streets of Port-of-Spain, a veritable melting pot of the races, a cheering crowd of Negroes, Indians and Chinese waved Union Jacks as she passed by while, above, banners hung across the roadway sang her praises.

Calypso singers, not to be outdone by the ringing of

hundreds of bicycle bells, chanted with warm, rich voices:

"We want to welcome wholeheartedly
Princess Margaret of the Royal Family
In Trinidad on the first of February
That will be a day in West Indian history."

They also sang:

"Lovin' sister of Queen Lilibet
Is Princess Margaret
She ent married, she ent tall
Like to dance, like to sing,
Like to try out anything,
If she been boy, she been King."

Margaret, in a cream dress, tiny pleated silk cap and diamond pin in the shape of an English rose, listened with interest as Sir Hubert Rance, Governor of Trinidad and Tobago, formally welcomed her and hoped that, "the rapid transition from the rigors of an English winter to the tropical climate of these latitudes" would not prove too trying.

He added that she "carried the growing burden of responsibility with all the unselfishness, grace and charm which are characteristic of the Royal Family."

That night Princess Margaret gazed happily from her windows at Government House. A thousand lights twinkled over indigo waters and far away she could still hear the beat of steel bands and ever-present calypso.

Trinidad really went wild over Margaret; political differences were forgotten and when she drove to San

Fernando through the politically important southern part of the island enthusiasm reigned where controversy had been. THRICE WELCOME TO THE SOUTH, OH DEAR PRINCESS, read a large bunting stretched across the highway.

At one point an estimated crowd of fifty thousand people jammed her route; sixty bell-ringing cyclists tangled together in a mass collision and it seemed a miracle nobody was hurt. Never has been seen so spontaneous and enthusiastic a welcome as the one Trinidad gave to Princess Margaret!

Of course she thoroughly enjoyed it, clapping her hands when a calypso band serenaded her with garbage can lids, oil drums and auto parts. It was one big happy carnival—and Margaret was the star.

As she drove in a motorcade of shiny black limousines to Port-of-Spain's ancient town hall, a hundred thousand people roared their greetings. It was deafening, but she never turned a hair. At Queen's Park Oval she drove in an open jeep wearing a pink silk dress, the skirt of which, in spite of the helpful hand of a lady in waiting, refused repeatedly to stay down.

Schoolboys in straw hats, brightly-colored jerseys and white pants performed the *bongo* in her honor, a local dance found chiefly in the seaside villages. A hundred girls wearing gaily-colored costumes and headdresses did the *bel air,* a dance with many intricate mincing steps. Then came a sudden rain storm and Margaret was nearly mobbed by the crowd running for shelter.

After church on her first Sunday morning spent in the West Indies, Margaret phoned her sister in England.

"What can you see?" the Queen asked.

"Bougainvillea, lemon trees, sea," replied Margaret. "And you?"

"Four inches of snow," laughed the Queen.

Later the Princess flew the eighteen miles from Trinidad to the island of Tobago, the fabled island which claims to be Robinson Crusoe's own. This is based on the fact that Daniel Defoe read up on Tobago and incorporated the data into his own narrative. From the top of the hill the Princess viewed historic Fort King George, surrounded by clear blue bays and gardens filled with yellow hibiscus, red poinsettias and purple-pink bougainvillea.

Back at Scarborough, the tiny capital where ships load their cargoes of cocoa and copra, Margaret boarded the *Britannia* and sailed into a rainbow-colored mist toward Grenada.

St. George where she landed sixteen hours later is one of the most beautiful towns in the whole Caribbean. It sprawls over a steep cliffside, and with its white-walled houses, red roof tops and slender church towers is almost Mediterranean in appearance. Around the shoreline are deep indentations, and behind these, lush tropical forests cling to the mountainsides. Nutmeg trees grow on the higher level and the golden fruit is exported in large quantities. Women sit cross-legged on the ground and with small mallets crack the nutmeg shells. The kernels then are dried and graded, while the pulpy part of the fruit is used for jam-making. The Princess was presented with a nutmeg-shaped brooch made by a London jeweler for the people of Grenada, who had sent him a real nutmeg as a pattern.

During her stay on the island the weather was showery but just the same she was able to see a great deal. She took her first dip in the Caribbean Sea from a secluded quarantine station beach. She would have preferred to bathe at the famed two-mile ribbon of sand but, because of hills in back which prevented privacy, she bowed to royal custom and swam alone.

Attending service in a church that was 127 years old, Margaret was watched by a thousand people who spilled out through the doorways and onto the balconies. One onlooker wore a T-shirt on which was printed the rather startling announcement: WISCONSIN—BIRTHPLACE OF THE REPUBLICAN PARTY. Two proud old men, former soldiers in an old West Indian regiment, stood rigidly at attention in their tight red and yellow uniforms as the Princess passed by.

The bishop of the Windward Islands, the Right Reverend R. N. Shaply, welcomed her to the crowded house of God with its bright red roof, yellow walls and the flag of St. George flying high in the breeze from its ancient tower top.

As she sailed away at nightfall two hundred men and boys holding flaming bamboo torches stood in the pouring rain to guide her yacht out of the semicircular harbor.

On a lovely Tuesday morning the *Britannia* rode northward through the green surf to the island of St. Vincent, with its volcano, *La Sulphiere*—the Sulphurous One. Among those welcoming the Princess were groups of golden-skinned Carib Indians, a handsome race of an almost Mongolian appearance.

A tableau depicting Captain Bligh of the *Bounty* and

the adventures he had while bringing the breadfruit tree from the islands of the South Seas to the West Indies was given in Princess Margaret's honor on her arrival at Kingstown, the capital.

There was something old world and eighteenth century about the surroundings, and the very polite Vincentians went so far as to hang out a banner reading: WE APPRECIATE YOUR VISIT—which they did.

Next day in Bridgetown, Barbados, special ceremonies were held in another Trafalgar Square where Nelson also graces a column. There the crowds were too awed to cheer. The Princess went sea bathing, using an air mattress for paddling in the water, and visited important sugar plantations.

In Bridgetown housing is a major problem, and during her visit to the Health Center Margaret inspected a table model of a rural dwelling with proper sanitation facilities that could be constructed for about $560. She drove back to Government House through more sugar plantations, a constant reminder that the island's economy is dependent on that commodity.

The Princess spent as much leisure time as she could spinning hot calypso platters during her stay. She started a collection to take home for the Queen. She also found time to pay a surprise visit to Bridgetown's Oval to meet the British Guiana and Barbados cricket teams who were engaged in playing a five-day match.

The Barbadons, led by their governor in his plumed pith helmet, waved the Princess good-by as she left their island. The crowds strained at the ropes around the quayside; foghorns blared; a schooner tipped to the deck line; and one too-enthusiastic spectator fell head-first into the water.

Through lines of fishing boats the Princess sailed into the harbor of Antigua. She was wearing a day dress of turquoise shantung with a full skirt, buttoned bodice and short sleeves, topped off with one of those chic little hats for which she's famous. This one was made of turquoise straw.

Two steel bands, Brute Force and Hell's Gate, performed with oil drums; the village choir at Willikies displayed fine technique in their singing. Richly dressed clowns led by twenty-foot-tall Christmas Carnival Long Ghosts rolled out the red carpet for Margaret, who by this time was getting used to all the varied surprises provided day after day for her amusement.

She made a safari to the old Leeward Islands station of the Royal Navy to see the "haunted cemetery." Many of the people buried there had died young—victims of the once-dreaded yellow fever.

The wooden houses at St. John's, Antigua, were freshly whitewashed and gleaming for the royal visit. On the Basse-Terre in St. Kitts, another of the Leeward Islands, the homes are of warm brown stone. In their excitement, cheering crowds ran into the surf to greet Margaret when she landed.

Leaving the Leeward Islands behind, she journeyed across nine hundred miles of blue water to Jamaica to spend five busy days. Hundreds of Americans were among those waiting to catch a glimpse of her. Visiting Spanish Town, she explored the most beautiful square in the West Indies, standing before the Rodney Memorial, built to commemorate George Brydges Rodney, who at the Battle of the Saints scored an important victory over the French.

During her stay on the island Margaret was introduced to many young people, and as she ascended the steps of the Senate House, recently opened by Queen Elizabeth, scarlet-gowned undergraduates formed her guard of honor. She attended service at the eighteenth century Cathedral of St. Jago de la Vege, mother church of Jamaica, and in Mandeville the children gaily chanted, "Ain't She Sweet."

At Port Antonio she rode down the Rio Grande Rapids on a bamboo raft with a grizzled barefoot captain to guide her passage. The thirty-two-foot raft had been specially built for the occasion, and was commanded on the eight-and-one-half-mile trip by Captain Red Grant who was chosen for the job because of his rating as a senior captain.

In Government House, Kingston, Lady Foot, wife of the governor, discovered Margaret to be a cheerful guest to have around the house. Once, hearing a sudden burst of song, she told a maid to "find that radio and turn it down," for she didn't want the Princess disturbed by the noise. A few minutes later the maid returned to say it wasn't the radio, but Princess Margaret who was singing in her bath!

Princess Margaret's successful Caribbean Tour took her into the coral archipelago of the Bahamas. Its inhabitants—disappointed because the Queen did not visit them on her own recent trip to Jamaica—feted Margaret with laughter and song. The children of Webster

Preparatory (Number one) School, some of them fair-haired and freckled, wore new white suits, blue sashes and red paper caps to recite:

"Hail Princess Britannia
Thrice welcome here today
With waving flags we greet you
And with right loyal hearts we say,
Hail Princess Britannia
Margaret so gracious and true
Deep our devotion as deep as the ocean
For we love you—we do."

Simple as the poem may seem, it expressed the thoughts of all West Indians for Princess Margaret. Little wonder they have suggested she be known in future as Princess Margaret of the Caribbean.

Margaret was on good terms with the press at all times during her trip. On her way to attend an engagement in Nassau she caught two women reporters sunbathing and told her chauffeur to stop the car.

The women looked rather sheepish but had to laugh when the Princess quipped, "What do you two mean by loafing in the sun when you should be out covering me?"

Emily Austin, for twenty-six years a maker of straw dolls and flowers for billfolds, had her own little Margaret episode to tell. Working one day in the straw market in Nassau, Emily looked up suddenly to see the Princess examining the wares on her stall.

Said Emily, "I just put out my hand like this and I touched her. I had one of these little dolls in my hand.

She smiled so pretty-like—and she took the doll. Oh, she's sweet, our Princess."

"Yes," chimed in one of Emily's co-workers, "she was so friendly. Our Margaret—we'd give her anything. We'd never think of charging HER."

Princess Margaret accomplished all—and more than had been expected of her on this first Caribbean tour. For one thing the friendly West Indians took the tiny smiling girl to their hearts. She did not go as a rival for the Queen's popularity but as a good-will ambassador for her sovereign sister. With no loss of dignity or decorum she was able to make the people feel she was one of them; that they were all part of one great family. This she did by entering wholeheartedly and without restraint into all the wonderful festivities they had so lovingly prepared for her coming.

The city of London proudly welcomed its Margaret home. Among waving flags and roaring crowds, the Princess drove to Mansion House where the Lord Mayor was waiting.

This was truly her day, and several old friends were on hand to greet her, including Lady Clementine Churchill, regal gray-haired wife of Sir Winston Churchill, then prime minister, who himself was prevented by a cold from attending the welcome-home luncheon, and Dr. Geoffrey Fisher, Archbishop of Canterbury.

Margaret appeared on Mansion House balcony with the Lord Mayor, a handsome figure in his robes and chain of office. She smiled happily as he called out for three cheers in her honor.

At luncheon the souvenir menu had a West Indian theme. It included a copy of the certificate declaring that in the year 1728 Ebenezer Polly was willing to "serve in his Majesty's Plantation in America, and that he is not over-persuaded, or enticed so to do, but that it is his own Voluntary Act."

A toast to the royal visitor was proposed by the Lord Mayor who said he could not help thinking, when Princess Margaret arrived February 14 at Antigua, that the enthusiastic welcome she received from the happy folk of that hospitable island was partly due to the fact that never before had they received "such a rare and sparkling valentine."

The Lord Mayor continued: "The power of Princess Margaret to win all sorts and conditions of men and women to her side is no regal artifice, but springs from those deep and abiding qualities of sympathy and humor which rejoice all hearts and serve the cause of solidarity and the brotherhood of all people."

After thanking the Lord Mayor and the Citizens of London for the honor they were showing her, Princess Margaret made a speech she had written herself and which she spoke from the heart: "I have been deeply touched since my return by the many expressions of good wishes which I have received. It is always a delight to be home after a long journey, and I am very happy to be here in London today. The ties which bind this great city to all the territories of our Commonwealth of Nations are strong and abiding. In the last five weeks I have seen sure proof of this in many schemes of development and progress in the islands I have visited. They will, I am sure, bring a growing prosperity to the whole area and contribute greatly to the welfare and happiness of all who live in the Caribbean.

"As I stand here in the city of London, my mind is full of the wonderful scenery through which I have been fortunate enough to travel during the past few weeks: of waving fields of sugar cane and graceful palms; of deep blue waters beyond the white coral sands and dramatic green hills thick with tropical vegetation; and the subtle rhythms of dancing and singing followed me wherever I went.

"But more vivid even than the colors of those lovely islands, or their music, there remains in my heart the memory of cheerful, friendly and most loyal peoples. Before I left for home I was able to send them a message of my deep gratitude for the wonderful kindness and hospitality which I received everywhere. I would like, on this occasion, to do so once again, and to thank them most sincerely for a very happy visit which I shall never forget. I am sure there are no peoples who are more proud of their British heritage, nor more eager to display their deep sense of loyalty to the Crown.

"I thank you, therefore, my Lord Mayor, both for the kind way in which you have received and welcomed me home and also for providing me with this opportunity of conveying something of the deep sense of appreciation I feel to those generous and warmhearted people whose guest I have been."

Chapter Sixteen

HER HEART'S TRUE LOVE

COME ON MARGARET, pleaded the headlines of a leading London daily, PLEASE MAKE UP YOUR MIND!

August 21, 1955, Princess Margaret's long awaited twenty-fifth birthday, was drawing near and speculation was mounting as to whether or not she would marry the divorced Group-Captain Peter Townsend.

Under the Royal Marriages Act of 1772 members of the British royal family cannot marry without the sovereign's consent until they become twenty-five. At that age they can marry contrary to the sovereign's wishes, provided that one-year's notice is given to the Privy Council. Within the year both Houses of Parliament are at liberty to disapprove the union, and if a marriage is performed in the face of such disapproval the royal personage forfeits all rights of succession for himself and his children, as well as all income granted him by the state.

In Princess Margaret's case her state income is six thousand pounds ($16,800) a year, which she derives from the annual Civil List. Parliament also passed legislation granting her an increase up to a total of fifteen thousand pounds a year ($42,000) in the event of her constitutional marriage.

At the time of her birthday Townsend was on leave from his British Embassy duties in Brussels, and on August 24 took part in the International Gentlemen's Horse Race, Ostend, Belgium. He had been termed the "innocent" party when he divorced his wife, Rosemary, in 1952. The former Mrs. Townsend later married John de Laszlo, son of the late Philip de Laszlo, portrait painter.

Queen Elizabeth, as temporal head of the Church of England, had sworn in her coronation vows to uphold the Church and its laws. The Archbishop of Canterbury, the genial and fatherly Dr. Geoffrey Francis Fisher, as spiritual head of the same church, was also discreetly opposed, by virtue of his position, to such a marriage between Princess Margaret and a divorced man. In fact the Archbishop had made his position public the previous February when he said: "The Church is right to exclude from marriage in church all, without exception, who have a former partner still living."

WHILE THE WORLD WAITS ON 25TH BIRTHDAY EVE . . . PETER TOWNSEND IS ON HOLIDAY WITH SONS ran the headlines in London's *Daily Mirror*. But even if the world waited in suspense, Britain's royal family, at least outwardly, were going about their daily business as if nothing unusual were happening.

A family party was in progress at Balmoral, Scotland. Besides the Queen, the Duke of Edinburgh, Prince Charles, Princess Anne and the Queen Mother, other birthday guests staying at the castle included the Duke of Kent, Prince Michael of Kent, Prince and Princess Georg of Hanover, the Master of Elphinstone and Dominic Elliot, son of the Earl of Minto. Princess Georg is the youngest sister of the Duke of Edinburgh.

The energetic Queen Mother was in charge of a bazaar to raise funds for building a new vestry at Crathie Church where the royal family worship when they are in residence at Balmoral, and she had persuaded both her daughters to help.

The Queen, at the wheel of her green Daimler, had Princess Margaret for a passenger as they drove to take over two booths at Abergeldie Castle. Both were in high spirits, laughing and joking together during their drive.

Margaret was delegated to sell nylons and nightgowns and, as can be imagined, did a roaring trade. Some of the gentlemen visitors were a little shy at discussing their purchases with the Princess. One finally found enough courage to ask for a pair of nylons.

"What size?" inquired the Princess, sensing his embarrassment, for he was blushing all over.

"I don't know," he answered rather lamely, "but they are for a young lady about your size."

"Oh," laughed Margaret, "that's easily settled. You'll want eights!"

On leaving the bazaar at the end of the afternoon, the

Princess caught her foot in a grass tuft and fell. Next day at church she was still limping. Dr. John Lamb, the Crathie minister, ended a prayer for the royal family by praying "especially on this day for Princess Margaret. May she always have God's guidance and with it find joy and peace."

Following her twenty-fifth birthday the Townsend affair simmered until October. As far as the general public was aware, she had not seen the airman for two years since his exile to Brussels, although it was rumored he had made one secret visit to England, and they had corresponded with one another.

On October 12 the airman was due to return to London for a month's furlough. The day came, and with it the beginning of eighteen suspenseful days as to the Princess's future status. At no time since the abdication of Edward VIII had British families been so divided on a single issue concerning their beloved royal family. However, interest in the romance was not limited to Britain and the Empire. It was world-wide.

Group-Captain Townsend arrived in London unshaven and looking very tired. He had driven across Europe to catch the air ferry to England. Usually courteous to the press, this time he was both curt and evasive.

Asked, "Will you meet the Princess?" he snapped, "I'm not answering questions like that. I've told you I'm just here for a holiday. I expect to be back at my job in Brussels in four weeks' time."

"Do you expect any startling development while you are here?" a reporter persisted.

"I am not answering questions of that kind," he said,

but when safe at last in his car and ready to drive away from the airport he regained his composure, put up his hands to ward off more questions and rewarded waiting photographers with a big smile.

Meanwhile Princess Margaret, her holiday at Balmoral over, boarded an express train at Aberdeen and, accompanied by her pretty young cousin, Alexandra of Kent, sped southwards to London.

Tension was mounting by the hour; people felt an official announcement was pending.

Much sympathy was in evidence for the Queen, whose lifelong devotion to her younger sister was well known. The Queen Mother found herself in the ironic position of never having received the divorced Duchess of Windsor only to find one of her own daughters placed in a predicament similar to Edward VIII's. Fate plays strange tricks—the Townsend Margaret romance had its beginnings in the Queen Mother's own home, although she is said not to have been aware of it.

The Princess reached London on the morning of October 12, and during the afternoon her mother flew in from her country home, the Castle of Mey in Northern Scotland. She drove immediately to Clarence House where Margaret awaited her.

At six that evening Peter Townsend drove up to Clarence House in his green Renault car. He was there until eight twenty, and on leaving was almost mobbed by a large crowd of cheering well-wishers and eager-beaver photographers. He made no statement nor did the authorities at Clarence House disclose whom he had seen.

He returned to fashionable 19 Lowndes Square, London, to the Marquess of Abergavenny's town apartment where he was staying.

It was obvious that much planning had been done in advance toward preserving the royal family's personal privacy in Margaret's first "official" meeting with Townsend since their separation, and other dramatic meetings to follow.

There was much criticism concerning the crudity of some stories appearing in the popular press, but even the most conservative of Britain's newspapers had at last been forced to admit there were real possibilities that Margaret and the air ace would marry, and that in so doing she might well renounce her rights of succession. Up to this time some of these newspapers had stolidly refused to admit there even was a romance.

Everybody now was asking, "Will she or won't she?"

The next day Princess Margaret took matters in hand and added fuel to the flames by driving to the home of her cousin, Mrs. John Lycet Wills at Binfield, Berkshire. At three in the afternoon Townsend left the Marquess of Abergavenny's apartment carrying two books and a leather riding jacket. Surrounded by clamoring reporters, all he would say was, "I am going away for the week-end, and I can't say where I am going."

He appeared to be in excellent spirits, and an old lady patted his arm and whispered, "Good luck, sir."

Townsend later turned up at the home of Mrs. Wills where he joined Margaret.

The same day the following statement was issued from Clarence House: "In view of the varied reports which have been published, the Press Secretary to the Queen is authorized to say that no announcement concerning Princess Margaret's personal future is at present contemplated. The Princess Margaret has asked the Press Secretary to express the hope that the press and the public will extend to Her Royal Highness their customary courtesy and cooperation in respecting her privacy."

At her cottage in Kingswood, Somerset, Mrs. Gladys Townsend, Peter's mother, said, "I cannot say what Peter's intentions are. If there is an announcement to be made when Parliament reassembles, then we had better wait until that day. Then we shall know."

In marrying without the approval of the Queen, it was generally thought that Princess Margaret would be obliged to renounce her rights of succession to the throne. The approval of the Commonwealth Parliaments would also be necessary if such a change were to be made.

A strong detachment of British police cordoned off the Wills home. They were equipped with walkie-talkie sets, radio motorcycles, police dogs and patrol cars. Princess Margaret wanted privacy and she was getting it. The Queen Mother was not far away. She had motored to Royal Lodge, Windsor, for the week-end. It seemed very likely to the romantically-minded that surely with Margaret and Peter spending the week-end together with friends, at last the long-expected engagement would be announced.

The next day Townsend was up early and drove to the home of Miss Norah Wilmot at nearby Binfield Grove. Miss Wilmot raises and trains horses, and the

Group-Captain, after selecting a three-year-old chestnut filly, went riding with the saddle boys. At the end of his canter he was once more stopped by a crowd of newsmen and photographers.

"I say, can't you see the horses get restive?" he shouted in vain, but the gentlemen of the press were out for a story. Finally he admitted Margaret wouldn't go riding that day. He looked relaxed and happy compared to the day he first arrived in England from Brussels.

On Sunday morning, October 16, a serious Margaret drove off to attend morning service with her mother at Windsor. Afterward, she returned to rejoin Captain Townsend in a car with closely-drawn blinds. A double line of police were required to control the crowd of three hundred as she drove through the gates. It was nightfall before the last of the curious left, and a van carrying four fresh police dogs arrived to take over.

Although nobody seemed to know what was going on in Margaret's rural hideout, things were far from quiet in the world outside. The *Manchester Guardian* and The Sunday *Times,* both respected British newspapers, took opposite positions on the contemplated marriage, The *Guardian* approving and The *Times* opposing it.

From the humblest home in the kingdom to the palace itself the pros and cons of the Townsend affair were being threshed out. One newspaper estimated the Princess had already gained the blessings and good wishes of almost fifty million people if she decided to marry him.

On October 17 Margaret and Townsend made their separate ways back to London, the Princess looking terribly sad and depressed. Britons who saw the pictures of her strained face in the papers were disturbed, for over the years Margaret's lively smile had been taken for granted.

Five hundred people cheered as she arrived at Clarence House, but if they were pleased with her behavior there were others who were not. Canon C. T. Kirtland, honorary canon of Canterbury Cathedral, speaking to twelve hundred members of the Mothers Union at Margate, Kent, an organization of Anglican churchwomen who vigorously uphold the sanctity of marriage and deplore divorce, said, in answer to a delegate's written question, "This is about the possibility of Princess Margaret's marriage. I would yield to no one in my loyalty to the Queen and the royal family. I think my feeling about the whole thing is one of profound sorrow. Here is somebody who is very dear to our hearts. Here she contemplates doing something which is deliberately an affront both to religion and the Church. I do not see what line the Church can take. The less we gossip about it the better. The Church cannot take in an innocent party."

British observers later described the statement as being the severest ecclesiastical attack on a member of the royal family since Edward VIII's abdication. Some papers took the Canon to task and called his words "most un-Christian."

The same evening Margaret and Townsend met for dinner at the home of Mr. and Mrs. Mark Bonham-Carter. This was the fifth evening the lovers had spent together, and what exactly would be the ultimate outcome was still as great a mystery as ever. Somber and unsmiling, Princess Margaret left the dinner party alone at one in the morning, and drove to Clarence House.

The scene temporarily moved to Denmark where King Frederik IX, after bidding good-by to Prince Philip who had been visiting him, reportedly said, "I know how it will end, and it will not end in the way you think."

Although the remark was important enough to merit an immediate official denial, the fact that the Queen of England's husband had been visiting with King Frederik gave it more than a small ring of truth. The reporter who overheard the King was positive he had heard correctly.

Meanwhile Margaret's family were arriving in London in time to play their own part in the pending climax.

Sir Anthony Eden, the prime minister, himself a divorced man who had since remarried, returned from the country and scheduled two Cabinet meetings for later in the week. The Queen Mother came home from Windsor. Finally, the Queen and her children returned from Scotland.

The eighty-three-year-old Princess Marie Louise, granddaughter of Queen Victoria, and Britain's oldest princess (she died in 1957), was reported as being opposed to Margaret's marriage to Townsend. A most democratic woman with a wit and sense of humor that almost matched Margaret's own, she declined to discuss such a thing on the grounds that members of the court were not allowed to give press interviews. She, herself, when twenty-seven years of age, had been divorced from the German Prince Joseph of Anhalt after nine years of unhappy marriage. She never took another husband.

Sir Winston Churchill reminded Princess Margaret of what had happened to the Duke of Windsor when he gave up his duty for love and advised her to "reflect." Like her regal sister, she had always admired the wisdom of Sir Winston and thought of the Windsors in exile— of summers in France and winters spent wandering in the United States, but never more than a few days at a time in England.

Margaret and Townsend continued to meet at the homes of mutual friends and at Clarence House. The failure of the palace press to give any guidance on the status of the romance was the subject of an editorial entitled, "A Damaging Silence" in the conservative *Daily Telegraph*.

The Prime Minister sent an urgent call to Sir Reginald Manningham-Buller, the Attorney General, to attend a Cabinet meeting. This in itself was unusual at such short notice.

Margaret's meetings with Townsend were made with the approval of her immediate family. They felt that after so long a separation the couple should be allowed to talk over their problems in private. The decision itself, as Townsend had said repeatedly, could not come from him. It had to come from Margaret. She and only she could decide whether or not they could go forward with their desire to marry.

The most lonely figure in all the deliberations was the Queen. Desperately anxious to help her sister, but with both hands tied because of her vows to church and state, she knew also that her husband was much opposed to Margaret's marrying Townsend. Philip felt that as he himself had made personal sacrifices in giving up his promising naval career for the goldfish-bowl existence as husband of the Queen, so should his sister-in-law be prepared to make similar sacrifices. He considered Margaret was in a way, letting him down.

The Archbishop of Canterbury—later to be most unjustly dubbed by many the "villain of the piece"—called on the Prime Minister. Officials declared that the meeting did not concern Margaret, although few believed them.

With the eyes of the world upon her, Princess Margaret stood quietly by and listened as her sister the Queen spoke at the unveiling of a statue of their father in Carlton Gardens, overlooking the Mall: "Much was asked of my father in personal sacrifices and endeavor. . . . He shirked no task, however difficult, and to the end he never faltered in his duty to his peoples."

Margaret may have thought that Elizabeth's message was meant just for her. She smiled faintly. It might well be that at that moment, Margaret's great decision was really made.

On October 22 the Princess drove into London's East End where the Cockney women call her "Our Maggie" and where she is especially popular. To the sound of deafening cheers she entered the Limehouse district. Women frantically waved home-made banners as she opened the new St. Nicholas and All Hallows Community Center at East India Dock. Policemen had to stand shoulder to shoulder in an effort to control the gyrations of the swaying crowd. "Good luck, Maggie. You marry him," yelled the crowd. It was one of those lovely, reassuring moments in life that Princess Margaret will probably always remember with gratitude. Afterwards she drove happily back to Clarence House for another tryst with Peter.

Like the Cockney women of London, from his home in Berkshire, Lieutenant Colonel Marcus Lipton, Labor member of Parliament also decided to speak his mind: "The public," he said, "is getting fed up with this long-drawn-out business. Apparently they love one another, and if someone is holding up a marriage, then let him say so. It may be the church, or somebody else. But anyhow, let's stop all this guessing."

When Parliament reassembled the following Tuesday, Colonel Lipton declared his intention to ask Prime Minister Eden "whether he will introduce legislation to repeal or amend the Royal Marriage Act of 1772." Colonel Lipton said: "The present government says it believes in freedom from controls. If it does, then it should abolish the out-of-date controls still exercised by the Royal Marriage Act."

The week-end of October 23 Princess Margaret spent with her sister and brother-in-law at Windsor Castle. With them she motored from the castle to attend morning prayer at the Royal Chapel in Windsor's Great Park. Then they returned to the castle.

For Margaret it was a day of reflection spent in surroundings filled with childhood memories. Here, as an evacuée, she had spent the war years with Elizabeth; here they had acted in pantomimes; and here like other children they had looked forward to the week-ends when their parents could come from bomb-torn London to visit them. Here her beloved Papa was buried in St. George's Chapel, where Grannie England, who always knew how to manage a crisis, had so recently been laid to rest.

It was only the second day out of the last eleven she had not met with Captain Townsend. He had stayed alone in London for the week-end.

In the House of Commons, which reconvened from its summer recess October 25, the question of whether the government intended to introduce legislation to amend the Royal Marriage Act was not reached during question period.

The London *Daily Sketch* complained: "How intolerable it is that the affairs of the British royal family should become gossip over every teacup in the world, a subject of offensive cartoons on the Continent and prizes in competitions in America and a text for busybodies in the pulpit. Advisers to the palace who allowed this situation to reach its present critical phase have a lot to answer for. Immediately, there is a pressing need for a clear statement about the situation lest more damage be done. The Throne must be protected."

Overseas in the Commonwealth, editorials were just as outspoken. Some were kindly disposed towards Margaret and her predicament; others were not. The Sydney *Morning Herald* suggested that if the Princess married Townsend the couple should retire into a "decent dignified obscurity." It complained: "Whatever reasons have led the Government and Palace to keep silent so long, the result has been little short of disastrous."

Margaret was also strongly cautioned by the sedate London *Times* in an editorial which said that if the Princess were married to a forty-year-old divorced commoner she "would be irrevocably disqualified from playing her part in the essential royal functions" and noted that hitherto she had played this part "with the utmost charm and devotion."

It was a compliment to Margaret and an example in personal self-control that she managed to continue her official duties throughout so nerve-racking a period. The knowledge that so many ordinary Britishers were genuinely sympathetic towards her, and the thousands of letters she received urging that she follow her heart's strongest desire, gave her comfort and the will power to carry on.

She traveled down to Seaford, Sussex, to open a school for five hundred invalid boys between the ages of seven and fifteen. Part of the twenty-eight thousand dollars needed to build it had been raised by the charity performance of Edgar Wallace's melodrama, *The Frog*, which Margaret helped direct, and which was badly panned by the critics. The Princess toured the new classrooms and talked to many of the children. Outwardly she showed but little of the strain and turmoil through which her own life was passing.

About this time Dr. Leslie Weatherhead, President of the Methodist Conference, issued a clear and rather sensible public statement concerning her fate. After so much bickering and gossip it was timely and welcome.

Said Dr. Weatherhead: "Princess Margaret and Group-Captain Townsend are popular young people in love with one another, and everyone would wish that they could have the right of any other young British couple and find happiness in marriage. But clearly the status of the Princess raises difficulties in regard to a fiancé who is divorced and whose wife and two children are living.

"Should anything—an airplane accident, for instance —unfortunately end the lives of Prince Charles and the Princess Anne, or if they both died without issue, then at Princess Margaret's death her eldest child would be heir to the Throne. Yet that child would be the fruit of a marriage which many Anglicans would not recognize as valid.

"This is bound to be a matter of vital public concern, for, among other things, such an heir would be doomed to disapproval or worse in the eyes of many of the people of this realm. If the State Church approved this marriage, it would break its own rules.

"If, however, Princess Margaret renounced all claim to the throne for herself and her issue, then she would be free, in the eyes of many, to enjoy married happiness with Group-Captain Townsend, though, even then, her example does not make it easier to uphold the ideal of Christian marriage in a land in which divorce is already too lightly regarded, homes too readily broken up and children too thoughtlessly deprived of the mental security of having two united parents, a security which surely is part of God's plan."

On October 27 the spotlight switched again to the Archbishop of Canterbury, and, as so much has been erroneously written in the press about this good and forthright man—with Mrs. Fisher, he was actually booed and hissed when his pictures appeared in London news reels during the climax of the Townsend affair—it is well to know something of his character and daily background.

Dr. Fisher is frequently confused with the notorious "Red Dean of Canterbury," particularly in America, yet there is no resemblance between the two. Once while visiting the United States the Archbishop was obliged to hand out printed statements in connection with his so often being mistaken for the Red Dean.

The human Dr. Fisher is a very able man. He was a public schoolmaster for eighteen years and is still apt to behave like one and make all his own decisions. His chaplains complain he does not give them enough responsibility, and often when somebody writes to one of them for an appointment with the primate, Dr. Fisher sends back a hand-written note to say he will see them.

He seldom prepares for a press interview and some of his quips are an editor's joy. He upset a lot of people when he described England's rising divorce rate as being "as beastly as Mau Mau." He called the new British commercial television "a lunatic agreement."

Dr. Fisher has always tried to be broadminded where love is concerned. His own son, Henry Arthur Pears Fisher, married Felicity Sutton, a Roman Catholic. The Archbishop did not attend the ceremony but his wife did.

Dr. Fisher loves America. He is a great friend of the Right Reverend Henry Knox Sherrill, Presiding Bishop of the Protestant Episcopal Church, and is usually asked to push the wheelbarrow in the Sherrill garden when staying with him. In Chicago he obliged newspaper photographers by posing riding a motorcycle! To the British royal family the Archbishop of Canterbury is their own minister and spiritual adviser. He marries them, buries them and baptizes their children. It was only natural that Princess Margaret should seek his help. The nation expected she would—and so did the Archbishop. On October 27 she did.

During the afternoon Princess Margaret was received by him at Lambeth Palace where he was awaiting her with books of reference and cross-reference pertaining to a problem such as hers. The Princess crossed the threshold of his study, stopped and smiled. "You may put away your books, My Lord Archbishop," she said, "I have already made my decision."

The curtain was falling on the royal romance. Margaret retired to Uckfield House in Sussex, home of Lord Rupert and Lady Camilla Nevill. Townsend was close at hand, staying at Eridge Castle, country seat of the Marquess of Abergavenny, elder brother of Lord Rupert and a close friend of the royal family.

Townsend was depressed and had begun to show signs of fatigue—a contrast to his earlier buoyant self. On October 29 he drove to the red brick mansion at Uckfield where the Princess and he walked hand-in-hand through the frost-covered fields. They were saying good-by.

The Queen and the Prince had gone to Scotland for the week-end; the Queen Mother was in Windsor. On October 31 the long-awaited decision came. Her personal message to the British people was one of quiet dignity and restraint:

"I would like it to be known that I have decided not to marry Group-Captain Peter Townsend. I have been aware that, subject to my renouncing my rights of succession, it might have been possible for me to contract a civil marriage. But, mindful of the Church's teaching that Christian marriage is indissoluble, and conscious of my duty to the Commonwealth, I have resolved to put these considerations before any others.

"I have reached this decision entirely alone, and in doing so I have been strengthened by the unfailing support and devotion of Group-Captain Townsend. I am deeply grateful for the concern of all those who have constantly prayed for my happiness.

"Margaret."

Chapter Seventeen

ADMIRATION, MORE RUMORS AND CRITICISM

For her courageous decision in renouncing Peter Townsend Princess Margaret received nothing but admiration and praise. From all parts of the British Commonwealth and the world, editorials were kind.

The Princess went right on with her endless task of visiting hospitals and fulfilling other civic duties. For a time rumor left her alone, then the British were in for another shocker. The story was circulated in the press that Princess Margaret had been converted to Roman Catholicism!

Two Spanish newspapers printed reports from Rome dated February 15, 1955, that Margaret might embrace the Roman Catholic faith. Buckingham Palace authorities bluntly stated: "No Comment," and the Duke of Norfolk, Britain's leading Catholic layman, described as

[140]

"sheer nonsense" reports that he discussed the conversion of a noted English personality with Pope Pius XII at the Vatican.

Margaret's deep devotion and interest in theological subjects had given birth to other such rumors in the past. One even said she would become a nun.

The correspondent of the Madrid Falangist newspaper *Arriba* said Margaret would like to marry King Baudouin of Belgium, a Roman Catholic. Both young people were twenty-five at the time. Although Britons generally took the story lightly, many Protestants in Canada and other parts of the British Commonwealth were very upset. Finally the rumor died a natural death.

In the spring of 1956 another story was circulating in London—and this one was considered important enough to merit instant denial by Buckingham Palace. This time rumor said the Princess would shortly be engaged to Prince Christian of Hanover, thirty-six, brother of Queen Frederika of Greece and a great-great-grandson of Queen Victoria.

The handsome six-foot-three prince served with a crack German regiment on the Russian front, during World War II, and later, after hostilities were ended, lived for a time in New York City. In 1954 he was in the limelight when he pursued a suspected purse-snatcher and his accomplice into Central Park, captured both with the help of a taxi driver and turned them over to the police. At the time of his rumored romance with Margaret he was employed in London by a shipping company, lived in a Baker Street apartment, and played for Blackheath Rugby Football Club. He was the rugged outdoor type Margaret was known to prefer.

However the denial came quickly: "The press secretary of the Queen is authorized to say that the report that Princess Margaret is likely to become engaged to Prince Christian of Hanover is untrue."

The prince also issued a statement: "I wish to deny the story that I might become engaged to Princess Margaret and to say that there is no truth in these rumors."

On May 12 the Queen invested her sister with the Insignia of a Dame Grand Cross of the Venerable Order of the Hospital of St. John of Jerusalem.

Margaret later attended the Empire Youth Service at St. Mary's, Portsmouth, where her old friend, the Reverend Simon Phipps, chaplain of Trinity College, Cambridge, was special preacher. Phipps, thirty-four, after a brilliant wartime record with the Guards, in which he was awarded the Military Cross for bravery, in 1951 entered the Anglican priesthood. To do so he renounced a promising military career and served as a curate at Huddersfield Parish Church. He is said to have helped Margaret in her quest for better understanding of theological matters. Apart from his ministerial duties, he writes the lyrics for popular songs. Margaret's fondness for modern music is another interest they share.

This interest in popular music was further satisfied when Margaret attended a jazz session given by Louis (Satchmo) Armstrong in London's Empress Hall.

"We've got one of our special fans in the house," growled gravel-voiced Satchmo, "and we're really gonna lay this one on for the Princess."

The audience gasped for there is an unwritten law that professional performers must refrain from personnally mentioning members of the royal family while entertaining them. But Satchmo wasn't disturbed by rules and regulations—he had Margaret in the house and was determined that she should enjoy herself.

"Yes, sir," grinned the famed trumpeter, "we gonna blow 'em down with one of those old good ones from New Orleans—'Mahogany Hall Stomp.' "

Margaret loved it. She clapped her hands enthusiastically and tapped her feet on the floor, but she didn't know Mahogany Hall was the name of the famed New Orleans brothel run by Lulu White!

Satchmo's performance that evening made protocol history. Not that he hadn't done so before while playing to her grandfather, George V, twenty years previously. On that occasion he announced "This one's for you, Rex." The old King smiled graciously and acknowledged the greeting.

The Princess was elected President of the University College of North Staffordshire, Keele, Newcastle-under-Lyme, succeeding Lord Harrowby who resigned on the grounds of age. He was a young ninety-one.

With Lord Terence William Span Plunket, thirty-two, an equerry at Buckingham Palace and a deputy master of Queen Elizabeth's Household to squire her, Margaret went to the Savoy to hear American singer, Lena Horne.

Again Lord Plunket escorted the Princess, but this time he had to share her company with the Reverend Simon Phipps. They all attended *Twelfth Night Revels,* given by the Sadlers Wells Opera Company, and between acts Margaret took time out to saw up a yule log cake.

With her Uncle Harry and Aunt Alice, the Duke and Duchess of Gloucester, she flew to Stockholm on June 11 to join the Queen and Prince Philip for the important equestrian events of the Olympic Games. Large crowds, mostly young women, lined the route near the airport to catch a glimpse of the visiting Princess.

Her twenty-sixth birthday photograph by Cecil Beaton showed Princess Margaret wearing a revealing one-strap evening gown of pink tulle. Now accepted as a world leader of fashions, Margaret found it was hard to please everybody, and much as her taste in clothes was admired, so at times was it criticized. A London newspaper complained indignantly when she was dropped from second to ninth place in the annual list of the world's best dressed women.

"Just who do these people think they are?" demanded the irate *Daily Mail* referring to the New York Dress Institute. "We pick the Princess," it added, and printed a picture of Margaret in full evening dress including a diamond tiara and sash of the Most Noble Order of the Garter.

The London *Daily Sketch* agreed with the *Daily Mail*'s opinion but the *News Chronicle* compromised by saying: "She has turned up at garden parties in draped silken dresses—but forgotten that they are sufficient unto themselves and do not need diamond brooches, fancy shoes, bracelets, pearls and frilly hats."

The uproar just went to show that which every American visitor to Britain should learn: only the British themselves are allowed to criticize their royal family.

Maybe the New York Dress Institute did have a point, for Winifred Munday writing in *Reynolds News,* another British newspaper, accused the Princess of having lost "her famous fashion sense." Complained the columnist: "Today we see her in head scarves, shapeless mackintoshes, cardigans knotted carelessly over her shoulders, wintry coats a size too big for her.

"The Princess even wore high-heeled shoes exposing all her toes, a bad style for anybody but a woman with perfect feet.

"Everything Princess Margaret wears is an advertisement for Britain's textile industries. In the past the advertisement has been good. It is no longer good. It is downright bad."

Poor Margaret. After reading that she must have felt like going about her duties wearing a placard: FOR EXPORT ONLY!

Chapter Eighteen

AUNT MARGO AND THE ROYAL CHILDREN

The telephone bell rang in the royal kitchen at Buckingham Palace, and when the receiver was lifted the chef heard a child's voice speaking. "This is Princess Anne. Please send me one large potato. I want to make a potato man!"

If Princess Margaret was a bundle of mischief as a little girl, then her fair-haired niece is doubly so. Full of life and bubbling over with curiosity at everything she sees, the little princess is growing up fast.

She loves her lessons, and even at seven years could write a tolerably good letter in longhand, was good at reading, composition and figures. She is now studying history, and all the traveling she has been doing lately on the Royal yacht *Britannia* is helping her geography a lot.

Not too long ago her elder brother, Prince Charles, was the instigator of most of the palace pranks, but not any more. With Charles away at boarding school, Princess Anne's the ringleader now.

Once the palace terror herself, Princess Margaret has stepped naturally into her favorite role—that of Aunt Margo.

There was no more exciting time for Prince Charles and Princess Anne than the afternoons when their mother's sister came to tea, or the happy week-ends they all spent together at Windsor. In spite of being a world fashion leader, Aunt Margo, no matter what she was wearing, got down on the floor to play cowboys and Indians with her small niece and nephew.

"More, Aunt Margo, please, just once more," they chorused together after Margaret had been captured and scalped. "Please Aunt Margo . . . You must die just once more." And Aunt Margo generally did!

If Princess Margaret copied her idol, the Duchess of Kent, then Princess Anne will certainly do the same of Margaret. Already she begs Aunt Margo to give her that outdated purse, or last year's hat to dress up in.

The Queen and Prince Philip are doing their best to have their youngsters lead normal lives, but it isn't easy. Living a goldfish-bowl existence has many disadvantages, and surely no mother in the world can be given so much "good advice" by well-meaning people on the upbringing of her children as is Queen Elizabeth.

"Is Prince Charles bored?" one mother wanted to know. "I think he attends too many polo matches," she complained. "Children get tired of looking at the same thing over and over again."

In this case the young heir to the throne wasn't bored. He loves horses, especially when his own daddy is riding one of them. When Charles was home all the time the weekly treat for the royal children was to see Prince Philip take part in his favorite sport.

Millions seem to regard poor Charles as their special concern, and once a London newspaper went so far as to demand: GET THAT CHILD A HAIRCUT.

When he learned to ride, one of his mounts happened to be a Russian horse, and one section of the press wanted to know: "Why can't he ride on a good English pony?"

Palace authorities have always dreaded those times when either royal child is sick, for remedies and cures pour in not only from well-wishers in England—but from all parts of the world.

Princess Anne is by nature a very generous little girl. She has been brought up to be kind to animals and has a pet dog and a white rabbit of her own. There are singing birds in her nursery, just as there were when it was occupied by her mother and Aunt Margo. She has been taught by Margaret to attend to her pets' needs, to brush their coats and, in the case of the dog, to see it is properly exercised. Aunt Margo sets her niece a good example in this, walking her own dog in the park.

Britain's youngest princess loves flowers and has her own little garden both at Buckingham Palace and Windsor. She weeds, hoes and digs, preferring to grow flowers to vegetables. Her beloved Grannie, the Queen Mother, is often treated to a special posy of Anne's flowers. On the Queen Mother's birthday Anne arrives early at Clarence House, carrying freshly-picked blossoms to brighten her breakfast tray.

To those "modern" parents who bring their offspring up from a book and never correct them in the old-fashioned way, it will come as something of a shock to know that when Princess Anne is naughty (and she often is) she is given a spanking. Nor is she allowed to have her own way with her parents or nurse.

Elizabeth and Philip spend all the time they possibly can spare from their royal duties with Anne—and of course with Charles during school vacations.

Philip has taught both his children to swim in the private pool at Buckingham Palace and they are both very good at it. They can ride their bicycles well and have ponies which were presented to them by the Russian leaders, Bulganin and Khrushchev.

Will Princess Anne be sent to boarding school like her brother when she is old enough, or will she always be tutored behind palace walls like her royal mother and Aunt Margo? Many Britons ask this question.

Prince Philip is known to favor schooling away from home for both his son and daughter. There are a number of excellent girls' schools in Britain and tomboy Anne would be in her element mixing with other children in one of them. The Duchess of Kent set a precedent by sending her daughter Princess Alexandra to boarding school, and her sons the Duke of Kent and Prince Michael were treated likewise. So were Richard and

William of Gloucester, the Queen's cousins. Certainly they haven't come to any harm.

However it would not be quite as easy for Princess Anne, second in succession to the British throne, to be just another pupil at a girls' school in the country. There would always have to be a plainclothes detective at hand to see that the little girl did not come to any harm.

It has been done however and in England, too. Princess Margrethe, heir to the throne of Denmark, has been attending school in Britain. Queen Juliana of the Netherlands allowed her daughters to have the benefit of mixing with other children in their own land. Crown Princess Beatrix is studying for a law degree at Leyden University.

Princess Anne, like her Aunt Margo, enjoys nothing better than meeting people. She was quite at home with the sailors on a recent cruise around the Scottish coast. The sailors in turn adored her.

"She's just like your own little girl," one man said. "Always getting into mischief!"

"How fast she grows," is the comment of those who see her pictures in the press. She is tall for her age and is inclined now to resemble Philip more than she does her mother. Her hair is golden and she has the same healthy complexion as her Scottish grandmother. Princess Anne was also the first British princess to wear slacks—corduroy ones!

What does she want to be when she grows up? Like most little girls of her age Princess Anne changes her mind from day to day. Sometimes it's a schoolteacher and then her dolls, of which she has many, are set up in a make-believe classroom. And sometimes it's a nurse. Then they are undressed and put to bed.

Before going away to school her brother Charles wanted to be a magician and do tricks like the conjurer did at his parties. He practiced a lot, but Anne wasn't very encouraging. She usually saw through his efforts, which was hard on a fellow eager to succeed.

Princess Anne enjoys going to church, but is allowed to leave before the sermon. She has been brought up from babyhood to hear—and now to read—something from the Bible every day. Elizabeth and Margaret were raised the same way, for their mother has always believed the Bible should be regularly read in every Christian home, and what is more, on view, not hidden away on a library shelf or used only on Sundays.

"Aunt Margo" is already getting competition as Britain's foremost fashion leader from her small niece. And Prince Charles is giving his father, one of Britain's best dressed men, a similar challenge in this field. Latest fashion note from Anne is a mink collar for her winter coat. She wears white gloves too!

Prince Charles was listed by a top British fashion authority as one of the eleven best dressed men in the world. Charles's wardrobe "has remained smart and imaginative as he has grown older" read the citation.

For all public appearances both Charles and Anne must look as if they have both stepped out of the traditional bandbox, with neatly combed hair and immaculate outfits. They have grown used to the stuffy royal cars whose windows must be kept closed to enable their occupants to reach destinations with every hair in place.

[151]

Princess Anne is already a veteran where flying is concerned. She has never been airsick and always asks to spend a few minutes out of each flight visiting the pilot's cabin. When visibility is good the view from the windows is a source of fascination for her. Both Anne and Charles thoroughly enjoy travel by boat, too, reflecting their father's love for the sea.

Now that Princess Anne is doing so well with her lessons she hopes to be allowed to take more trips to museums, art galleries and other places of interest in London.

Before each new birthday Princess Anne cleans out her toy closet. The discards are then carefully painted and mended by staff members of Buckingham Palace and sent to London's Great Ormond Street Hospital for Children. Only the matron knows which toys belonged to the little princess and she is sworn not to tell. The hospital is the one to which James M. Barrie, Princess Margaret's friend, bequeathed all royalties from his play *Peter Pan.*

Anne enjoys playing with boys. She is always happy when her second cousins, Richard and William of Gloucester, and Michael of Kent, come visiting during the school holidays. The Gloucesters with their tousled fair hair have plenty of adventures to relate to the eager-eyed princess. Richard, before going away to school, was a cowboy fan and loved to dress like Hopalong Cassidy. Like Sir Winston Churchill, he is an amateur bricklayer.

Describing herself recently, Princess Anne said, "I can write. I can sew. I can bathe myself. I take my puppies

Whisky and Sherry out for walks." With these accomplishments Princess Margaret's niece is doing all right.

Queen Elizabeth makes it a rule that, even when the governess is with Princess Anne, it is herself or Philip who disciplines her. Anne is good-mannered and obedient and is allowed plenty of freedom when out walking with her parents, often straying quite a distance from them.

Since Charles left home Princess Anne has shared her lessons with Carolyn Hamilton and Susan Babington Smith. They take turns at clearing up the schoolroom at Buckingham Palace and do their lessons in the morning. At present Anne's favorite subjects are history and poetry. Elizabeth and Margaret often remark to each other how pleased their grandmother would have been over this. Anne enjoys reading adventure and travel books but, with the exception of *Peter Pan,* fairy stories are not much in her line. *The Twins*—a series of books by Lucy Fitch Perkins—are currently among her favorites. They tell of the adventures of twins in many countries.

At midday the three girls leave the schoolroom for recreation in the grounds of Buckingham Palace. There they cycle, climb trees with the aid of ropes, or "keep house" in a real gypsy caravan. Piano lessons, dancing and gymnastics take up most of the afternoons. During week-ends spent at Windsor Princess Anne likes to go riding on Wise Old William, a very special horse. The Queen Mother and Aunt Margo often come for tea with Anne during the warm summer months. At such times the little princess entertains them in her caravan.

As yet neither Charles or Anne takes part in public duties. On trips aboard the royal yacht they are taken to places of interest when the Queen and Prince Philip go ashore to attend an official function.

Although the Queen tries to keep both children out of the public eye as much as possible, she does allow them to meet the Commonwealth prime ministers and other important dignitaries who from time to time visit the palace. In that way she feels they are unconsciously learning a most important part of their future duties.

On May 5, 1958, Princess Anne found herself a patient in the Hospital For Sick Children, Great Ormond Street, London, for the purpose of having her adenoids and tonsils removed. This was another democratic gesture on the part of her parents, for normally a special hospital ward and operating room would have been set up in Buckingham Palace.

Prince Charles is enjoying his boarding school life at Cheam, a preparatory school at Newbury, Berks, founded about 1640. He had previously attended Hill House School, Knightsbridge, with much success in spite of the hordes of photographers and inquisitive crowds who used to wait for him outside. Cheam is his father's old school. Lord Randolph Churchill, father of Sir Winston, was another scholar.

It is the first time the heir to the British throne has gone to boarding school as an ordinary student, and the Queen asked that he be treated exactly like anybody else.

At first some boys resented him because his presence subjected them to endless interrogation by relatives during the holidays. They wanted to know every little detail about the young heir to the throne. However, Prince

Charles has overcome this "difficulty" and is now quite popular with his fellow students. He is good at lessons and, like Anne, enjoys history best. At Cheam he also studies Latin, French, algebra, geometry, English and other subjects. Like his father, he has a great sense of fun and an insatiable curiosity. Later special instructions in constitutional history and civics will be necessary to prepare him for the future. The Prince is most enthusiastic about football and cricket.

There are ninety other boys at Cheam and the fees amount to about $850 a year. The desks are heavily scored with boys' initials and the beds the ordinary serviceable kind one would expect to find in a boys' school.

"I don't believe you'll be able to bounce about on that bed," Queen Elizabeth told her son when they first visited Cheam together. This remark prompted the offers of free beds for the entire school from several of Britain's leading bed manufacturers! SHOULD THE PRINCE SLEEP ON A HARD BED? ran the headlines in one newspaper. A HARD MATTRESS WILL BE GOOD FOR HIM, decided another. The offers of new beds were promptly refused.

On the subject of caning, Peter Beck, one of the joint headmasters said when asked, "If Charles misbehaved, would he be caned—and where?" replied, "In the usual place." This remark was greeted by much approval by people all over the country.

When Prince Charles contracted pneumonia he shared a sickroom with four other boys. On December 19, 1957, he completed his first term at boarding school and left to spend the Christmas holidays at Sandringham, where a very curious Princess Anne was waiting.

Chapter Nineteen

ROYAL RIVAL

In 1956 Princess Margaret found herself with a very friendly rival—the eighteen-year-old Princess Alexandra of Kent.

All the blue-blooded young bachelors in Mayfair society were clamoring for a spot in "Alexandra's Band" as her confidantes were known. A few months back all they had wanted was the chance to get into the special "Margaret Set." The younger princess was even partnered by several of her vivacious cousin's beaux.

Princess Alexandra, one of the three children of the elegant fashion leader—and Margaret's idol—the Duchess of Kent, had inherited her mother's classic looks, brains and good taste in dress. She was also, like her mother, one of the least wealthy of Britain's royal family.

When her father, the Duke of Kent, was killed while on active service with the Royal Air Force in 1942 his allowance from the state died with him. Her mother received a pension of 398 pounds a year (approximately $1,120.62), which is exactly the same as that allotted to any other air commodore's widow with three children. The Duke left an estate valued at $444,122.61 out of which the Duchess and her family derive some income from interest incurred, but most of the capital has to be held in trust for Alexandra's elder brother, the present Duke of Kent.

The Duchess has often had to sell antiques and jewelry to make ends meet. Her mother-in-law, the late Queen Mary, and her brother-in-law, the late King George VI, helped her at times. It was not until comparatively recently that the British newspapers revealed the low state of her finances.

In spite of living on a small budget, she has never shirked a single public engagement since her husband's premature death. She even went to Communist-infested Malaya as a morale-booster to the inhabitants and planters who were living daily in dread of Communist raids on their homes. The Duchess and her son, the young Duke, traveled around Malaya in an armored car and more than once narrowly escaped being ambushed.

Alexandra likes to do her own shopping and prefers buying custom-made dresses and suits directly from the best London stores to having them made by court-appointed dressmakers. She loves color and has never had to battle for the right to wear what she liked as Elizabeth and Margaret did.

Princess Alexandra was also able to enjoy more freedom from the public eye than her cousins. Most of her childhood was spent at Coppins, Iver, Bucks, a lovely old country house left her father by his aunt, Princess Victoria. There with her two brothers, (the younger, Prince Michael George Charles Franklin was named for President Franklin D. Roosevelt who was one of his godfathers) she lived the life of any other country child, playing in the fields and taking long walks through the quiet lanes.

She doesn't wear much make-up, and only since a visit to Paris "to complete her education" has she adopted a more sophisticated hair style.

Alexandra loves jazz and, like other British debs of her age, had her own signature tune—"Ain't Misbehavin'." Her mother owns one of the best collections of modern jazz and calypso records in Great Britain. Margaret and Alexandra copied her example and now have collections of their own.

Marina, Duchess of Kent and her debutante daughter make the prettiest mother-daughter team in Britain's royal family. With their flawless features and chestnut-brown wavy hair, they stand out in any crowd.

The Duchess of Kent at the time of her marriage to the fourth son of King George V and Queen Mary was one of Europe's great beauties. When Queen Mary told her husband of the romance he laughed and said, "George has chosen the most beautiful princess in Europe—and the poorest!"

It was a real love match, and the British people gave Princess Marina of Greece the greatest welcome extended to a royal bride in generations. The wedding in Westminster Abbey in 1934 even outshone that of Princess Elizabeth and Prince Philip (Marina's first cousin) who were married at a time when Britain was still living under austere post-war conditions.

The Duchess of Kent, daughter of Prince Nicholas of Greece, is related to most of the royal houses of Europe. Her father, during his exile in Paris, had tried to eke out a living as a painter. The Duchess herself is good at portrait painting.

Since the time the chic Marina Hat was named for her she has always been noted as one of the most fashion-conscious members of the royal family. The Duchess of Windsor and, more recently, Princess Margaret have been her only rivals in this field, yet she has never spent large sums on clothes. Her budget, especially since her husband's death, would not allow it.

The Duke and Duchess of Kent were the story-book Prince and Princess come to life. They were truly in love, and the young Duke never ceased to be amazed at his beautiful wife who could speak seven languages, was a cosmopolitan and yet enjoyed nothing more than to bathe her own babies in the nursery at Coppins. Their home was always open-house to relatives and friends. The Duke of Windsor was especially close to the Kents.

When the Duke of Kent was killed in an air crash over Scotland his widow was disconsolate. Queen Mary realized something had to be done right away about his beautiful "Mara," as he called the Duchess. The aging Queen went quickly to Coppins where she persuaded the Duchess that for the sake of the children and her late husband's memory, she had to carry on. The Duchess did, as her public works show, especially in the field of nursing and public welfare. In the County of Kent she is especially loved.

At the close of World War II, she made a lonely pilgrimage to Scotland and walked across the moors to the spot where the Duke's plane had crashed. Every week she had gone into the dark burial vaults beneath St. George's Chapel, Windsor, to lay a bouquet on her husband's casket. Later King George VI allowed her to have his body buried outside among the flowers and trees.

Now the Duchess lives for her children and her work. She has kept her good looks and her figure, so that when she is carrying out some public engagement with Princess Alexandra they might easily be taken for sisters instead of mother and daughter.

Princess Alexandra has enjoyed meeting her mother's wide circle of friends, who include such celebrities as Noel Coward, Danny Kaye, Sir Laurence Olivier and Vivien Leigh. Elizabeth and Philip did much of their dating at Coppins, the Kents' home.

Alexandra is good at cards and can play backgammon with the best. With the young men in "Alexandra's Band" she has earned the reputation of being both witty and a good companion. She is a television, movie and ballet fan as well as a good typist, and is also taking a course in nursing.

Alexandra and her cousin laughed off the newspaper stories they were rivals, for Margaret thinks too much of Aunt Marina to feud over popularity with her daughter.

Of cousin Margaret, Alexandra once remarked, "She can never forget she is a princess for one moment."

Chapter Twenty

THE HOURGLASS FIGURE

The magnificent state coach rumbled over the paving stones at Buckingham Palace taking the Queen of England to open her Parliament, and as it passed through the great iron gates the London crowds first gasped with surprise and then cheered, for inside, sitting proudly beside her sister, was their own beloved Princess Margaret.

Queen Elizabeth had created a precedent and had flouted royal tradition. There had been some opposition in court circles to Prince Philip's riding beside her on ceremonial occasions, let alone her sister. However, Princess Margaret had earned the honor of riding with the Queen to the opening of Parliament. She had also won her independence.

Margaret had just returned from the most difficult good-will journey of her life, taken to East Africa at the time of the Suez crisis. The whole thing had exploded over her head and Margaret, who was visiting Moslem dignitaries, could easily have added more fuel to the flames. She confided later to friends that she had been constantly afraid of saying something that would involve the British Crown in a dangerous controversy. Nobody could have been more diplomatic and she returned in triumph to a grateful England. Only a year before she had publicly renounced Group-Captain Peter Townsend for reasons of duty and faith.

Regarded by many as the Queen's best "ambassador," Margaret has an advantage over Philip; she is not married to the sovereign! Philip had been on a world tour lasting three and a half months, made because senior court advisers thought he was getting too popular.

Margaret's daily London routine has altered considerably since *l'affaire* Townsend. She is still required by convention to live at home with her mother because it just wouldn't be right for a young, unattached princess to set up an establishment of her own. However, she does have her own front door! Dignitaries visiting the Queen Mother at Clarence House seldom have the pleasure of meeting Margaret as well, for the Princess is not as readily available as she used to be.

Of course, when she is at home she still takes meals with her mother, but nowadays they don't often go to a play or movie together for they have different tastes. Once Margaret would say, "Oh, I couldn't leave Mummy,"—but now all that is changed.

One drawback to living at Clarence House with her mother is that she cannot invite anybody in to lunch or dinner whenever she likes, for her mother might be entertaining in the dining room—and after all, the Queen Mother is the lady of the house.

The Princess with the hourglass figure still endeavors at all times to be the most consistently best-dressed member of the royal family. She is lucky that nature endowed her with such fine proportions. Weighing one-hundred pounds, she is five feet one inch tall and she uses make-up specially adapted to her clear complexion and pale skin. She frequently changes her hair-styles and in so doing she has disproved the theory that royalty should have conservative hair-dos.

When Princess Margaret first appeared at a West End theater with her hair worn in a sophisticated urchin cut, some of her immediate family were horrified. Short soft waves close to the head replaced the curled long bob she had worn since childhood. Women who saw her at close range remarked that the new hair-do suited the Princess. "It makes her look taller and younger," somebody commented from the crowd.

She dresses with tact, first trying out each new garment at home, paying particular attention to the way it reacts to various postures. Once on a royal tour the wind blew her skirt over her head and she's never forgotten it!

Most of Margaret's daytime clothes are designed by Stiebel, although those she likes to wear at home are often made by Miss Ford, one of the royal dressmakers. Hartnell still makes her evening gowns, particularly the kind she needs for great and official occasions. Others for less formal appearances are designed by Desses and the establishment of the late Christian Dior. The frill-and-bow hating Princess carefully goes over fashion sketches submitted her, and at times pencils in her own suggestions.

She doesn't have to battle for the right to wear what she likes as she did in more youthful days. A hundred yards of ivory tulle went into the dreamlike ball gown she ordered from Dior in Paris when she paid a visit to his salon in 1949 on the way home from her Italian holiday. She wore it as a surprise to a London dance where its strapless top caused a great sensation. Never before had a female member of the British royal family been so daring, although all the gentlemen present were full of admiration for both the dress and the wearer.

Not so Margaret's father. Next day her photographs wearing the strapless gown were in every newspaper, and he insisted straps be added before she wear it again. Although temperamental Margaret wept, her tears and coaxing were all in vain. She was furious when she next saw her precious French creation plus the addition of straps. "Now it looks so old-fashioned," she stormed.

Today things have changed at the court, so much so that November 29, 1957, both Princess Margaret and her sister wore what were described in the press of two continents as "the most daring evening gowns of their social careers." Luckily they did not appear together at the same function.

Queen Elizabeth attended a reception among the white-haired elders of the staid British Museum wearing a full-skirted dress of white tulle cut low in front and back, precariously secured by two tiny jeweled straps that hugged her sleek white shoulders.

While her regal sister was appearing in London, Princess Margaret went to the University College of Staffordshire students' ball. She was in a good mood, dancing waltzes, rumbas and even a hot American jive number. Eleven handsome students had their morale lifted when they were selected to dance with the Princess. She made it more informal by asking the band leader to play three change-partner numbers. At two-thirty the next morning, the merry Princess was still dancing.

Contrary to what most people think, the Queen's sister owns little jewelry and never wears rings. Most of the royal jewels are family heirlooms and belong to the Queen. Margaret has three pearl necklaces of which she is very fond, while her favorite earrings were a gift from her sister. Unlike Elizabeth's, Margaret's ears are not pierced.

From time to time she has received jeweled regimental badges from the units of which she is colonel-in-chief, and is much attached to the floral diamond sprays presented her by the peoples of Rhodesia and New Zealand. She has one small tiara for use only on special state occasions, for by convention unmarried girls do not wear them.

Trade buyers around the world study just what she is wearing for they know that thousands of fashion-conscious women will want to copy her styles. In the great stores of New York's Fifth Avenue, dresses are sometimes tagged "Princess Meg Models."

She is particularly aware of color and her favorite shades range from pale pink to cherry red. To Norman Hartnell she once said, "Please, Mr. Hartnell, create me a gown like the foam on a cherry tree"—so he did.

After World War II she introduced many young British women to the "new look." Nipped-in waistlines, soft rounded shoulders and long curving skirts suited her admirably. Every year since she has made her own special contribution to the world of fashion. One spring it was the "long line" which she modified as she saw fit, still keeping the short full skirt and low waistline.

Margaret's choice for evening wear is frequently influenced by the brilliant sash of a royal order which often has to be worn across it. This explains why so many of her gowns are white. These special evening dresses are never worn very often, and when their usefulness has been served, pearls, rhinestones and other precious trimmings are carefully removed. Then what is left of the gown is burned.

Clothes of state must never be worn by anyone not entitled to do so. Margaret's day clothes are just as carefully guarded, and, even when she tires of them, are never given away. The risk of their being commercialized and thus imperiling royal dignity is too great. Instead, they are taken to pieces and the material sent to charitable organizations.

Of course the Princess wears her older dresses in the privacy of Clarence House, especially if she is expecting to work extra hard at her desk. She does not discard her tweeds. Year after year they come out for the Scottish holidays at Balmoral and the Castle of Mey. They are also useful for certain days at the races. On such informal occasions her favorite is a gray tweed skirt with side pleats. She also has a stand-by in a three-quarter-length natural cashmere coat worn with a bright silk scarf tied at the throat.

She loves silk headscarves, particularly those printed with amusing decorations. They are kept on a shelf of her wardrobe in a specially labeled box.

Princess Margaret was the first member of the royal family to wear a calf-length evening dress, and today when dining at home never wears the full-length kind. For after theater parties spent in some off-beat night club she has an array of informal dresses including an all-black creation with halter neckline and short full skirt.

When she was a teen-ager, a black evening gown once led her into hot water with the press. She wore it for the first and last time to a movie premiere only to read in a newspaper next morning that the writer wondered if it had once belonged to a woman of forty. Since then she has chosen black gowns only when they are cut to youthful designs.

During the winter months Margaret bows to the damp English climate and frequently wears velvet—warm ruby or mole-colored creations for day use, complimenting them with full-length coats which occasionally are fur trimmed.

Suits she seldom wears, for she finds the two-piece ensemble more practical. The small coat can be left behind when she has to dine at some official function, especially if the dining room is centrally heated. However, she does possess one elegant tweed suit in gray, with a jacket trimmed with black braid, which she uses exclusively for train or air travel.

"My hats must be me!" is a favorite expression of Margaret's—and by that she means they have to be gay.

Flowered hats she loves. Her favorite, designed for the first Caribbean visit, she christened, "Quite bliss." She has a good face for wearing hats; its oval contours and clear-cut features are suited to nearly every current style. Margaret made the coolie straw famous, and at the same time gave herself some relief from the hot sun while still obeying the maxim taught her by the Queen Mother: "A royal face must always be seen."

Unlike other women of her age, Margaret can seldom go shopping in person. When she tried it recently in Charing Cross Road vast crowds gathered and traffic was stopped. Instead she attends long private sessions with her dressmakers who bring with them sketches of new designs and samples of material.

If she attends a fashion show at one of the well-known salons, anything she takes a fancy to is immediately withdrawn from the collection before it is viewed by the general public. She must never have the disastrous experience of appearing at an official function only to find another woman wearing a gown identical to her own.

Of course, in spite of what the experts call Princess Margaret's sixth sense (clothes), she sometimes stuns them badly by deliberately violating the very rules of fashion she knows so well. Recently, the costume she wore to the Hurst Park races shocked quite a number of them. Although the stylists criticized her, they admitted being intrigued by her unconventional get-up which was expertly described as follows:

"A stocking-like goblin hat of heavy soft material, a short cloth coat with mannish lapels and a fur collar, a dress of different material from the coat—yet shoes and dress have large matching black buttons, suede shoes, suede handbag, but . . . but . . . PIGSKIN GLOVES!"

Three of London's leading fashion experts gasped.

Said Number 1: "It seems a strange blend of town and country wear, and neither is the right thing for a race meeting. You can't mix suede shoes and suede handbag with pigskin gloves."

Said Number 2: "The coat is too short for an ordinary coat and not short enough for a short one. To my eye the collar is wrong and the lapel line is not at all smart. However, it's daring of her to wear it."

Said Number 3: "I can't follow the style. With that tunic it's essential that the dress should be of the same material. The Princess defies the rule. Yet she's matched the buttons. Extraordinary, to say the least, and different."

As a footnote they should have added that Princess Margaret also wore a string of pearls and had two winners.

Chapter Twenty-one

REGAL QUEEN

Margaret's sister, Queen Elizabeth II, was recently described as the world's most regal queen. She is also a very human one.

Living continually in the public eye, where even the smallest action may be misconstrued, her life can hardly be called a normal one although she tries to make it as normal as possible. A stickler for discipline and devotion to duty in the traditional pattern set by her grandmother, she finds a time and a place for everything.

Part of each day is set aside for her daughter, Princess Anne—and for her son Prince Charles, too, when he is home from boarding school. She joins in their games, reads aloud to them and takes them for walks in the palace grounds. Week-ends spent at Windsor are always a family affair, but the greater part of her time is always taken up with the exacting job of being queen.

Her official residence, Buckingham Palace, is the home of her childhood and full of memories. She learned to darn a pair of stockings and, like her sister Margaret, was taught to keep her room tidy, though it is doubtful if she has ever found it necessary or had the time to darn Philip's socks!

She ascended the throne better qualified than any other monarch in the nine previous reigns, with the exception of Edward VIII, now the Duke of Windsor. Her father had allowed her to read many secret state papers while she was still in her teens, and when she took his place at the Trooping of the Color in the summer of 1951, he was as proud as any parent on his daughter's graduation day.

On her twenty-first birthday she said: "I declare before you all that my whole life, whether it be long or short, shall be devoted to your service and the service of our great imperial family to which we all belong."

Elizabeth meant it!

Her marriage to Prince Philip was a love match, and broadened her whole outlook on life. The girl reared behind palace walls learned much from the young man who'd mixed with the masses.

Most men would have resented the fact that as queen his wife must always take precedence over him, especially a man who has lived far from the spotlight of world events—but not Philip. He has adjusted himself to being husband of the Queen and in turn has earned a great measure of respect from the British people. The press have often commented upon his intelligence.

However, Philip is master in his own home. He knows just when to humor Elizabeth—and how to get her to laugh. In Scotland a gillie on the Balmoral estate overheard this little story: Philip was waiting for Elizabeth to go walking on the moors but the skies were dark and rain seemed to be threatening. The Queen couldn't make up her mind whether to accompany her husband or not. Philip's patience was going fast. "Oh, come on, you silly old sausage," he snapped—and—the "silly old sausage" did!

After marrying Elizabeth, Philip made it his business to make an extensive study of world conditions, especially in the field of industry. In Canada he has delighted the people on his visits with his intimate knowledge of their postwar boom. In Britain he even presided at the first meeting of the Royal Mint Advisory Committee when it was concerned with designing the new coins for his wife's reign.

Queen Victoria once wrote of her consort: "Albert helped me with the blotting paper when I signed." Philip, however, isn't content merely to use the blotting paper; he has more than a will of his own. Even Elizabeth is used to the not-so-royal quotes the newspapermen love to glean from his speeches but, unlike her great-great-grandmother Victoria, she does not say, "We are not amused."

Philip's most famed speech was made before an audience of Britain's foremost scientists who were more than a little surprised at the knowledge it contained. The

Queen's husband had been burning the midnight oil in order to study up on his subject.

For Britain's dowagers his most shocking remark occurred at the time when, like Bernard Shaw's Eliza Doolittle, he used the swear-word "bloody" in public. He was a banquet guest of Edinburgh's Royal College of Surgeons. At the end of a presentation speech, president Walter Mercer turned to Prince Philip and said: "May it please Your Royal Highness to accept this bleeding cup."

Accepting the cup, a relic of days gone by when surgeons bled their patients for every kind of ill, Philip replied very seriously: "I can only say it is bloody good of you."

On another occasion, speaking to newspapermen, many of whom had spent weary months trying to get some kind of explicit guidance on how to cope with what were then only rumors of Princess Margaret's romance with Peter Townsend, he said of a recent newspaper strike: "I found it a most interesting experience—breakfast seemed to take no time at all. I must confess that I only really missed the strip cartoons."

Then he specifically mentioned three points in connection with reporting on the royal family's activities. He said that members of the royal family were "slightly different from" other public figures because they are "public figures for life." Other celebrities, such as presidents, film stars, politicians and even TV personalities, have what he called "their periods of obscurity."

Secondly, he maintained that in the case of "ordinary people, which we are," the more one is quoted and reported "the less one is inclined to leave to chance both what one says and what one does in public, and the more jealous one becomes of one's private life."

The result he declared to be "very dull" and often made the royal family appear "rather unenterprising" to newspapermen.

"Remember," he continued "that our mistakes, instead of sending us into obscurity, are never forgotten, although, of course, they may be forgiven."

Thirdly he said official royal tours might tend to become boring to some newsmen because each visit seemed to follow almost exactly the pattern of the last. He asked them to remember that members of the royal family were unlikely to visit the same place more than once in five years, and for local residents it was not "a dreary repetition."

Like Princess Margaret, Philip has a way with the young. Addressing two thousand children on a recent world tour he had them in stitches when he recalled that the natives of New Guinea called him "fella belong Mrs. Queen."

On anniversaries Elizabeth receives white carnations from her husband, just as she found them waiting for her on their wedding morning. She also gets a piece of jewelry which Philip chooses and sometimes designs.

Elizabeth has learned from experience not to hurt the feelings of the man in the street, and particularly to leave nobody out. Once in Basutoland, Africa, she noticed a group of girl guides isolated from others who were meeting her. Against the advice of officials, she immediately walked over to greet them. They were patients from a leper colony!

In Rome during an eightsome reel—one of Elizabeth's favorite dances—a young Italian nobleman, unfamiliar with the intricate steps, tripped and fell at Elizabeth's feet. Picking himself up, he was full of apologies, but she immediately put him at ease by saying, "Please don't apologize, because I thought I had tripped you and it was my fault."

A group of American debutantes were recently having difficulty fixing on their tiaras. "However shall I keep this on my head?" asked one, as she examined herself in the powder room mirror.

"Use bobby-pins," piped a cheerful voice from the rear. "I do." The girls gasped. It was Queen Elizabeth.

During a royal tour, Elizabeth and Philip were riding in an open jeep when Elizabeth rose to review the troops. Philip stood up as well and was promptly told by his wife to sit down.

Elizabeth, unlike Queen Victoria, is very fond of horse-racing. She first registered her colors when she was Princess Elizabeth, and not since the reign of her pleasure-loving great grandfather, Edward VII, has any British monarch had so many horses in training as she. Edward's mother, Queen Victoria, disapproved quite openly of her son's love for the "sport of Kings." Queen Elizabeth's mother obviously does not mind for she races horses too.

However Elizabeth has strong views on other matters, such as the red-coated guardsmen who stand on sentry duty outside Buckingham Palace. Too many beautiful tourists had their photographs taken making faces at the sentries, with arms around their waists or even kissing them—the poor guardsmen standing rigidly at attention, unable to resist their advances. The Queen soon put a stop to this; pictures of sentries are now only permitted if they are standing by themselves!

Elizabeth isn't as meticulous with her tours of inspection as she was when a princess, for they often led into embarrassing situations. Once word got around that she was to pay a surprise visit to a battleship and the men were ordered to make things spic and span for the occasion. A dingy ledge was hastily "done over" with gray paint and when Elizabeth came to that particular spot, she ran her gloved hand along it in search of dust . . . Instead, she ruined her glove!

At a well-known officers' training school she called attention to a cadet whose belt buckle was unshined. The young man was called up and rebuked, but the powers that be at Buckingham Palace were later told in a tactful sort of way that Elizabeth need not be so severe in her inspections.

The women do not always escape Elizabeth's eagle eye or tongue either. When she caught a friend powdering her nose in the palace corridor, she snapped, "This is not a cloakroom!"

Queen Elizabeth inherited the quick temper of her father's side of the family but has now learned to control it. As a child she would take Margaret's provocations only for so long before exploding.

Nobody could be more considerate of her employees than Elizabeth, and when she first came to the throne, she insisted on working out a plan that would enable them to spend more time with their families.

On a fine evening when the royal chores are nearly

over Philip often walks Elizabeth in the beautiful grounds of Buckingham Palace. Right in the heart of busy London they have forty-five acres of lawn and gardens. In the middle of their five-acre lake is an island where, as little girls, Elizabeth and Margaret pitched tents and played cowboys and Indians. Their greatest regret was their parents' refusal to let them camp out for the night.

Queen Elizabeth keeps up the gardens at all the royal residences as best she can. As a child she had a little garden where she grew snapdragons, but had to leave it behind when war came and she was evacuated with Princess Margaret to Windsor.

Every day when the court is in residence a truckload of fruit, flowers and vegetables grown in the royal kitchen gardens at Windsor is driven to London. Feeding guests is a problem for any housewife and Queen Elizabeth can never take them to a restaurant.

The Queen is always surrounded by her dogs; she even took one on her honeymoon. Her special breed of corgis, descended from Welsh sheepdogs, are not as popular with other people in the palace as they are with the Queen. One of them bit a visiting bishop and another tried his teeth on a Grenadier guard!

American news photographers gave Elizabeth quite a shock when she visited the United States, although later she learned to laugh when they yelled "Hi, Highness!" At one time she was more surprised in her own country to notice British newspapermen standing with cameras at their sides, making no attempt to photograph her as she passed. The men had earlier been refused permission to take pictures of her in a railway station, and retaliated by refraining from doing so when she left the building. The refusal had not come from Elizabeth personally.

Many favorable comments have been received on this side of the Atlantic pertaining to the Queen's new streamlined appearance. Philip persuaded his wife to diet in order to reduce her weight, and she has never appeared more attractive than she does today.

She is also more interested in current fashions and for this she has her husband and Margaret to thank. Gone are the days when she copied her mother and wore nothing but pastel shades. Now she sports reds and greens and other dazzling colors.

In January 1958 Queen Elizabeth made fourth place in the New York Dress Institute's annual poll. Most delighted was Princess Margaret, who wasn't even mentioned.

Chapter Twenty-two

THE PRINCESS AND THE ARTS

Noel Coward once said that had Princess Margaret been born anybody else she could easily have earned her living on the stage. This is probably true, for all her life she has been deeply interested in the theater.

Her voice is exciting. She sings in rich deep tones. Her rendition of "La Ronde de l'Amour" delighted Greta Garbo. Plays are generally sure of a large boost in their box-office sales if the Princess attends a performance. She prefers to sit in the stalls where she can study technique and stage direction. On more than one occasion she has been criticized for flouting tradition by refusing to watch, lonely and aloof, in the royal box.

She has even dabbled in the theater and, like many

others in the business, was given a bad time by the drama critics over a play she helped direct, although in a single performance it grossed $8,840 for charity.

Presented at La Scala Theatre, London, the thriller play was Edgar Wallace's *The Frog*. Margaret assisted Alan Jefferson in staging it, and during the first performance moved freely about in the audience. Afterwards she sat up until three-thirty in the morning in a Leicester Square night club to await the reviews. These described *The Frog as* "appalling . . . amateurishly bad . . ." and "pedestrian. . . ."

Despite bad notices the Princess turned up next evening with her mother and sister who were cheered by a crowd numbering several hundred. However, since then Margaret has forsaken directing.

Among her intellectual friends are John Synge, thirty-three, great nephew of the famed playright J. M. Synge. A good-looking art expert, he has been one of her friends since she was twenty. When Synge dates Margaret for the evening she is taken first to a movie, then to a small restaurant in off-beat Soho where they discuss the latest books and paintings until the early hours of the morning. When Synge co-authored the play *A Priest in the Family* Margaret read it long before it went into production. A number of her suggestions are said to have been incorporated into the script.

The London publisher, Mark Longman, is another whose stimulating company she enjoys. In recent years he has been responsible for discovering and encouraging many young writers.

Rory MacEwen, a Scot, plays the guitar at her parties.

Author Julian Fane; actress Joyce Grenville, whose take-offs of British society grand dames are enjoyed as much in New York as in London; and John Cranko, the Royal Ballet choreographer, are other artistically-minded friends.

Margaret attended the final rehearsals of Cranko's revue, *Cranks,* and later discussed the material with the author. It opened to rave reviews in London but flopped in New York.

She finds an outlet for her own frustrated talent for the theater by association with its stars.

The Princess is a prolific letter writer and a British newspaper editor has said she would make a better-than-average woman journalist. She keeps diaries of all her tours abroad and makes home movies, too. These provide amusement for her immediate family and have helped Prince Charles and Princess Anne enjoy their geography lessons better.

She has written a number of short stories for her nephew and niece, but it is doubtful that tradition may be broken so that other children may enjoy them.

In 1954 she became the first British princess to win a crossword puzzle contest and was delighted with her prize—$8.82 worth of books. The crossword editor of *Country Life* magazine suspected a hoax when the signature of the Queen's sister turned up on a winning entry, so the powers-that-be were immediately contacted. "Yes, she did it," they confessed; "in fact all the royal family are very keen on crossword puzzles."

Although her mother is an enthusiastic collector of modern paintings the Princess goes in more for the traditional. The latest portrait of herself, painted by a forty-seven-year-old Florentine named Pietro Annigoni, has already stirred up a hornet's nest of controversy. The Princess likes it, which is really all that matters, and has allowed it to go on public exhibition.

One critic called it "a new Mona Lisa" while another hoped that "future generations would not be tempted to judge either Princess Margaret or twentieth century painting in England from this portrait." The artist declared he had painted the Princess "as a woman of mystery, not completely understood by anyone." He described the greenery in the painting as symbolic of her "royal cage" and the white dress and dark stole as representative of a "dual personality." He said he had tried to incorporate into his work Margaret's "mystic, religious quality."

The portrait took a year to finish and the Princess gave thirty sittings either at Clarence House or in Annigoni's Kensington studio. Four years before, he had painted the Queen for the Worshipful Company of Fishmongers. Everybody was pleased, and a member of the court saw fit to comment, "It is obvious Annigoni found the Queen a straight, simple person to paint."

Margaret's personality turned out to be more complex a matter, but the sitter was pleased; Philip, Elizabeth and the Queen Mother, who had commissioned the controversial portrait, were delighted. The Queen Mother paid two hundred guineas ($588) to the artist—only a token fee. He refused to accept more as he was anxious to paint the most exciting princess of the century.

When the painting was nearly finished somebody was needed to act as stand-in for Margaret, to wear her gown and hold the folded stole, which one art critic has compared to melting toffee. Georgina Moore, a London show girl, was chosen for the job. Later when friends found out some dubbed her "The Body" and others "Eliza Doolittle." Although Georgina never actually met the Princess she is grateful for the "break" which Margaret and Annigoni gave her. All the publicity has helped her stage career.

Sometimes called "the Elvis Presley of the art world" by his contemporaries in the field, Annigoni since the day he painted Queen Elizabeth has been the most sought-after portrait painter in Europe. He mixes his paints with eggs, wine and varnish as the artists did in the lush era of the Renaissance. He also manages to insert a tiny portrait of himself into the background. In the case of Elizabeth he is shown rowing a boat; in Margaret's picture his profile lies hidden among the leaves.

Princess Margaret is definitely interested in the arts and would take a more active part if she were able. The world would be richer if it were allowed to read some of her writings and see some of her Aunt Marina's exquisite little portrait miniatures, or the Queen Mother's outstanding private collection of modern paintings—but alas, royal taboos say that we may not.

What a stir in America Sir Winston Churchill's paintings made, yet there were some people on both sides of the Atlantic who did not think it proper that this colorful side of his personality should be publicly shown.

As we all know thousands of people—some who had never been inside an art gallery before—turned out to see them. Princess Margaret's little stories might similarly delight the children of the world.

Chapter Twenty-three

CASTLE OF DREAMS

The Queen Mother discovered a dream home for herself and Margaret in an atmosphere of bleak remoteness.

A desolate coastal road winds over the moors to Barrogill and the few trees to be seen are bent by storm and wind. The fairy tale fortress, then called Barrogill Castle, with its turrets pointing upwards like witches' caps, fascinated the Queen Mother right away.

A hurricane had stripped slates from the roof only the winter before; much restoration was needed. It wasn't the kind of place one would expect a queen to fall in love with—but she did. Immediately she went to work arranging the transformation of the centuries-old structure, renaming it the Castle of Mey.

Princess Margaret was delighted with the purchase. She decided on a color scheme of rose and white for her own private suite which overlooks the lonely majesty of the Pentland Firth. Then there was a nursery to plan for Prince Charles and Princess Anne who would most certainly be summer visitors.

Only four hundred yards away from the castle gardens is Peedy Beach, probably the most exclusive beach in Scotland, where the royal children can build their sand castles away from inquisitive eyes.

It was this complete privacy that attracted the Queen Mother and Princess Margaret to the Castle of Mey. They did not care that electricity, telephones and main water were nonexistent when they first took over the property. A home in Scotland where they could rest from royal duties and walk unattended in the countryside was something they had always dreamed of.

The Queen Mother called in a local architect, H. S. McDonald, of Thurso, to draw up plans for the renovations, and a very wonderful job he did. Above all, both women wanted to modernize the castle without spoiling any of its historical features. The stone spiral staircase, which has proved so exciting to Charles and Anne in their games of hide-and-seek, and which becomes so steep and narrow near the top that it has to be negotiated on all fours, has been kept absolutely intact.

While repairs were going on, the Queen Mother and her daughter went shopping in the neighboring towns. Their finds included a gray enameled gun case and a tiny writing desk fringed with a neat brass rail. They also found two red plush chairs with gilt-covered woodwork and a set of three beautiful green plush armchairs.

The Queen Mother's favorite buy was a series of nineteen prints by William Daniel that cost her only $3.75 each. He sketched them one hundred thirty years ago while sailing around Scotland's rocky coasts. Even queens and princesses like to find a bargain when they go shopping.

Princess Margaret often takes a stroll to the roof-top to enjoy the magnificent panoramic view of the red cliffs of Orkney rising sheer out of the sea twenty miles away. At night the friendly winking lighthouses in Pentland Firth, where the Atlantic and North Sea currents boil as they meet, claim her special attention.

Like all genuine old fortresses the Castle of Mey even has its ghosts—two of them.

In the eastern tower is the famed haunted room where a sixteenth century Earl of Caithness is said to have imprisoned his daughter because she had fallen in love with a farm boy. One night when the wind howled over the battlements the tormented girl flung herself to the courtyard below and was instantly killed. Villagers will swear that her apparition known as "the Green Lady" has haunted the Castle of Mey ever since.

There is another ghost, this one dating from our own times. During World War II a soldier serving with the Black Watch shot himself in the castle. It is said that whenever the bullet hole which he left in the wall is filled up the plaster falls out.

Because of her close connections with the land of the heather Princess Margaret was recently the subject of a rather startling suggestion—that she be made Queen of Scotland! Even Edinburgh's staid and serious newspaper the *Weekly Scotsman* backed the idea. In fact it devoted two front page columns to the topic and it is not one of the sensational type of newspapers. It declared that such a change would placate the pride of the Scottish nation and so establish happier relations with England.

The article further stated that Scottish life would be greatly stimulated if Princess Margaret made her home as Scotland's queen at Holyrood Palace, and observed that the English sovereign might write her sister accepting vacation invitations to be spent at Balmoral.

Most famous female sovereign of Scotland was the ill-fated Mary Queen of Scots who, like Princess Margaret, was always in hot water because of her romantic inclinations. She was married three times, first to the Dauphin of France—later Francis II; secondly to Henry Stuart, Lord Darnley in whose murder, February 10, 1567, she was thought to have been implicated; and thirdly to the divorced Lord Bothwell, whom most people believed responsible for blowing up Husband Number Two with gunpowder.

Mary was forced to flee into England, where she claimed protection from Elizabeth I, who imprisoned her for eighteen years and finally executed her October 25, 1586. By a stroke of fate the rival queens rest peacefully side by side in London's Westminster Abbey.

Margaret and Elizabeth have heard of the suggestion to make the Princess Queen of Scotland but future generations must wait to find out if they commented on it in their diaries.

Chapter Twenty-four

LITTLE MOTHER

There is a lovely story they tell of Princess Margaret in Trinidad. After being presented to the Princess a native official remarked, "Madam, my people are unwashed and unshod."

Very softly she replied, "They are my people, too."

Princess Margaret is fascinated by ordinary men and women and the way they live. Like her grandmother she likes to pay surprise visits to families not on the royal itinerary. She enjoys getting a birds-eye view of an everyday home where hours of preparation have not preceded her coming.

"Forgive me for barging in on you like this," she apologized to one astonished British housewife, "but I wanted to visit a family that had not been warned to expect me."

She also likes a truthful answer to any questions she may put to officials of countries she is visiting, embarrassing though they may be. For instance, in Trinidad she was curious about the wages earned by native workers. She was promptly told by an official they were low because the hot climate eliminated the need for fuel and warm clothing.

Margaret raised her eyebrows and remarked, "That sounds a bit too glib for me."

When formal tours tend to drag she will take upon herself the task of livening them up. In Antigua she stopped a whole cavalcade of cars to chatter gaily with some old women she noticed carrying baskets of newly-picked cotton.

She is a conformist by nature but is annoyed when she finds she has unconsciously been the cause of other people's discomfort.

Recently when she was returning to London from Scotland the Tay Bridge station was closed to everybody save passengers. A certain Mark Patterson was unable to bid good-by to his sister who was leaving for Kenya. Peeved, he wrote Princess Margaret and within ten days—something critics of the royal family should note —he received in reply a formal apology. She was extremely annoyed with British Railways and promised nothing like it would ever happen again.

Sometimes a royal tour is twelve months in the planning. Split-second timing is necessary; itineraries must be prepared; officials go on ahead to work out plans with local authorities in the countries to be visited.

One must never forget that Elizabeth II is not just Queen of England. She is queen of all the countries of the Commonwealth and as such is expected to visit them at intervals. It would be physically impossible for her to attend every important function, such as the first opening of a new parliament, in person. Often a royal relative goes in her place. For instance her aunt, the Duchess of Kent, journeyed to Ghana for the opening of its first parliament; and Princess Margaret for the inauguration of the West Indies Legislature.

There are also state visits to be undertaken to other countries that do not form part of the British Commonwealth. The Queen and Prince Philip have in recent times paid such visits to Portugal, France, Denmark and the Netherlands. Sovereigns or heads of these countries pay similar visits to Britain.

Then there are the good will missions such as that undertaken by the Queen Mother to the United States in 1954. Sometimes such a visit will do more to ease hurt feelings than a score of politicians are able to accomplish. Britain was still smarting over the Suez affair when Elizabeth and Philip visited Washington, Jamestown and New York, winning admirers all along the way.

Princess Margaret started her royal tours early. Her first, to South Africa in 1947, was a particularly happy one since it was a family affair undertaken with her parents and sister. Peter Townsend was also in the party but the Princess was still a schoolgirl and the romance that one day would startle the world was then undreamed of.

Traveling on H.M.S. *Vanguard,* Margaret felt very grown-up with her own stateroom furnished in green chintz covered with pink rosebuds. With Elizabeth, she delighted the people of South Africa. She also made a few hearts beat faster by swimming out of her depth in the Hickman River and having to be rescued.

She grew used to the tiring monotony of official receptions, handshaking and long speeches. She knew what it was to feel her wrist painfully aching from greeting dozens of loyal well-wishers.

In addition to her first outstanding tour of the Caribbean Princess Margaret has made other successful royal journeys. One of these was taken with her mother to Southern Rhodesia at the time of the first speculation over the Townsend romance. She looked tired and worried and at one point had to give up altogether and let the Queen Mother go on without her.

Royal tours tire her quickly and change in climate makes her an easy victim of colds and stomach upsets. In Southern Rhodesia she caught a bad cold but recovered enough to fulfill at least some of her engagements.

The Rhodes Centenary Celebrations were in progress when the Princess and her mother arrived at Salisbury, capital of the self-governing colony on July 1, 1955— in that country a brisk winter's day. They were driven down historic Third Street, popularly known as The Royal Mile, and the procession included a mounted escort of British South African police carrying lances with fluttering pennants of blue and gold.

Later they left in the Royal Train for Bulawayo, its fifteen freshly painted ivory white coaches gleaming in the sunshine. Their apartments were located in three air-

Princess Margaret is greeted by a former polio patient at a charity concert in London.

Group Captain Peter Townsend

Princess Margaret arrives at the Royal International Horse Show to watch the competition for the King George V Gold Cup.

Princess Margaret arrives at Government House, Ottawa in 1958, with her host, the Governor General of Canada, Vincent Massey.

*Princess Margaret leaves the Diamond Jubilee Hall in Mombasa
after receiving the gold filigree garland which she is wearing.*

During her 1956 tour of East Africa Princess Margaret inspected this game farm near Arushna.

Princess Margaret, escorted by Billy Wallace, attends a Halloween Ball in London.

Simon Phipps—the Chaplain of Trinity College in Cambridge and a close friend of Princess Margaret.

conditioned coaches used for the earlier South African tour.

Arriving after an overnight journey, they made another triumphal procession through cheering crowds. Two little girls managed to elude the police lines and dashed out in front of the royal car to give the visitors personal gifts which the smiling Queen Mother leaned forward to accept.

In one African village three women dancers were so fascinated with the Princess that, leaping high in the air, they threw themselves at her feet and serenaded her with high-pitched greetings. Margaret, who was desperately trying to cope with her cold, took their show of enthusiasm in stride and accepted the Basuto grass hat a young girl offered her.

Southern Rhodesia's official gifts to the visitors were diamond brooches made in the form of Rhodesian flame lilies. Three and a quarter inches long and made of platinum set with three hundred small diamonds, they are valued at three thousand dollars each. The designs were modeled from an actual lily bloom, Gloriosa Superba, flown to Johannesburg and quickly sketched before it wilted.

The Princess wore a gown of royal-blue organza over tapestry for a special garden party at which pioneers and widows of pioneers of the territory were presented. They included two Dominican nuns, one of them then eighty-nine years old, who had performed many heroic acts of nursing under most primitive conditions.

Great satisfaction was felt among the Rhodesians at the last-minute decision made by the Queen Mother and Princess Margaret to join the procession to the grave of Cecil Rhodes situated high in the Matapos. It was a never-to-be-forgotten experience; the long line of cars threaded themselves like a snake up the mountainside while thousands of people waited patiently on the great round Kopje at the top. Among them were some who had actually attended Rhodes' funeral and a few who could still remember the surrounding countryside before he ever saw it.

The Queen Mother and the Princess were warmly applauded as they took their seats near the flat granite slab which marks Rhodes' tomb. A biting wind whipped across the rocky plateau, making it difficult for the Queen Mother to keep her ostrich feather hat in place. The Princess, wearing a rose-beige coat, shivered with the cold and many people remarked that day how really ill she looked.

Pipes wailed at intervals during the forty-five-minute-long service at which the royal visitors sat with the Misses Violet and Georgia Rhodes, nieces of Cecil Rhodes, who had flown from England to attend the centenary celebrations.

The Queen Mother's and Margaret's wreaths were placed close to the inscription on the tomb which simply reads: "Here lie the remains of Cecil John Rhodes."

Before leaving Bulawayo to go to the Rhodesian midlands the royal pair paid an informal good will visit to Luveve, an African village. There, the Queen Mother impulsively stopped the car and, with Margaret, called on Mrs. Betty Banda, a member of the Red Cross Society. They were very much interested in her home and re-

marked on a dressing table cover made of an old newspaper cut into intricate patterns.

A triumphal archway had been erected at the village
entrance with a slogan reading: GREETINGS GREAT WHITE
QUEEN AND GREAT WHITE PRINCESS. Among the Africans
waiting to be presented was Chief Mzimuni of Gwanda,
whose people had recently given 529 bags of grain to
help feed the anti-Mau Mau forces fighting in Kenya.

Squatting on the ground, fifteen Chopi Timbila
musicians in bright costumes entertained with their
primitive instruments made of hollowed gourds and
chanted a modern folk song. They sang an old song of
greeting that has been used for many years in East Africa
and the Belgian Congo. Then the famed Johannesburg
Jubilee Singers joined in the program, their songs including one of greeting that had been composed to
mark the royal tour of 1947. It asked for a blessing on
"all descendants of Queen Victoria."

The climax of the program was a gala performance of
Pageant of Rhodesia by Christopher Ede. Then, ignoring
the clouds of dust, the Queen Mother ordered the shades
of the royal car pulled farther back so that the crowds
would be able to get an unobstructed view as she and
Princess Margaret drove to the railway station.

Ten thousand Africans gathered in the hollow square
at Gwelo, Southern Rhodesia, where with thunderous
shouts of *"Balete"* they accorded Margaret and her
mother the royal Zulu salute. This was on July 7 and on
July 9 the Queen Mother unveiled a memorial to
Kingsley Fairbridge, one of the first Rhodes Scholars to
attend Oxford.

Cecil Rhodes in his will provided for the establishment of the famous Rhodes Scholarships which provide funds to enable selected students in the United States, the British colonies and Germany to study at Oxford University, England. Thirty-two of these scholarships are available to students living in the United States.

Later the royal party drove up the steep mountain road through scenery ablaze with scarlet and purple blossoms to famed Christmas Pass, so named by the pioneers who first camped there, Christmas day, 1891.

Umtali itself is a booming modern town full of new houses, industries and eight Christian churches. The visitors spent their time looking at typical houses and African Women's Clubs. The women themselves were surprised at the real interest shown.

Next day Margaret's cold was worse than ever; the wintry weather and brisk east winds had taken their toll and, much against her will, she agreed to let her mother continue the tour without her. Suffering a slight temperature, she was left behind at the Leopard Rock Hotel.

Towards the end of the African visit, when she had recovered, a visit was made to the African village of Mrewa on the Mangwende Reserve. There Margaret laid the foundation stone for an African women's clubhouse, the first of its kind in the country. It was organized by the wife of the chief.

Fifteen thousand Africans, many of the women sitting on the ground with their offspring, cheered the visitors, their yodel-like cries echoing again and again through the granite hills.

An agricultural show was in progress at Queen

Elizabeth Hall, and there, resplendant in rich scarlet robes was Chief Mangwende himself. The royal car was delayed by the chief's official jester, who, flourishing *assegais* and a battle ax, first performed a solo dance before conceding the right of way.

In a speech of his own composition, the chief began to speak.

"Mother, welcome," he began.

"Twice we have been honored by Your Gracious Majesty to enter our humble country and walk amongst us. It is good. Welcome, Mother of our gracious Queen and British Empire in which space and distance have become of small account when words and works may encircle the globe as does the sun, so that no part of the Empire may brood in darkness."

Then the proud chief turned his attention to Princess Margaret. "Welcome also to the daughter of our honored Empire," he addressed her. "Thus has our dream come true that royalty should cross our threshold."

Outside in the world, the Africans' deep affection for both royal women did not go unnoticed nor did the fact that the Queen Mother spoke so often of the advancement made by the two races together.

"Little Mother, little Mother," the people of Mombasa, Kenya shouted in their native Swahili tongue when Princess Margaret arrived to commence her important East African tour, September 23, 1956.

The visit came at a time when the Suez crisis was nearing explosion point. She was expected to meet not only Africans and Asians, but members of Arab communities. One false word on her part might easily have involved the royal family in an international incident. As usual, Margaret, with her tact and charm, emerged with flying colors.

Her program was a heavy one and had evoked criticism in Britain. It was whispered that some of Margaret's relatives thought that so busy a schedule would help lessen her heartache over Peter Townsend.

Among Margaret's personal staff was René, the French hairdresser who was with her on the first Caribbean tour. On that occasion his outstanding coiffure was the regal Empress Josephine style dressed high at the back and worn with a tiara. However hot and sticky the African weather might become, Margaret's hair arrangements had to be perfect.

Mwangavu which translated means The Radiant One, another name given her by the people of Mombasa, wore a new hair-drier hat to a special get-together of Arab, Asian and African women where Indian dancers hung garlands of golden blossoms around her neck.

In welcoming Margaret, Mrs. Sondhi, president of the Indian Women's Association spoke of their "silver binding of common abiding affection for the Royal Family."

The Princess was especially intrigued with the history of Mombasa, originally a prosperous Arab and Persian settlement, and visited by Vasco da Gama on his first voyage to India in 1497.

In a dress of pale yellow taffeta, and looking the very symbol of the twentieth century, she visited with veiled women at the home of the Liwali of the Coast, the Arab administrator, Sheikh Mbarak Ali Hinawy. The women, all of whom observed the ancient purdah custom, were covered from head to foot by black robes. They watched Margaret through narrow slits in their veils. It was hard on male reporters, for this was one time they could not attend. The women, who had hidden their faces from men from the time they were young girls, lifted their veils to be presented to Margaret.

The Princess was greeted by the Liwali's wife and taken to a first floor reception room. Here, while dream-like *dhows* passed a stone's throw from the wide windows, the Princess drank black Arabian coffee, ate dates and sweetmeats and was given rare perfumes and incense. The Liwali's wife presented her visitor with a miniature sword, a replica of those worn by Arab nobles.

Another Arab leader, Sheikh Mahfoud Mackawi, wholeheartedly greeted Margaret, although he had been one of the leading advocates of severing all British connection with the Kenya coastal strip and returning it to the Sultan of Zanzibar. He even built an archway that bore the words: MACKAWI GREETS PRINCESS MARGARET.

Hers was the first royal visit made to Mombasa since the Duke of Windsor's in the thirties and for everybody it was a great occasion. Hundreds of people in the crowds broke rank and ran after her car. Africans feasted on roast oxen and danced into the night.

Throughout Kenya it was VK Day, for Margaret's visit symbolized the end of four years of bitter struggle against Mau Mau terrorists.

More excitement was in store when the *Britannia* sailed into Port Louis harbor, Mauritius. As Margaret landed, crowds no longer able to restrain their excitement broke down police lines and ran to touch her car for luck. Officials feared for her safety as the auto rocked from side to side. Even the Princess later said she felt a bit nervous.

The local police were upset over the unruly behavior of the crowds and contended that Margaret's own refusal to have a motorcycle escort was largely to blame.

Said one irate policeman, "We bought nine new motorcycles especially for the royal tour. Then came word from Buckingham Palace there must be no motorcycles." He scowled. "Apparently the Princess objects to their noise."

In Dar-Es-Salaam, officials responsible for organizing the royal visit were taking no chances. They persuaded Mrs. Lenni Brown of New York City, whose husband Robert W. Brown had been studying African tribal law, to help them.

"You are just the person we are seeking," they explained. "We want someone the same size as Princess Margaret to test our arrangements. Get in that jeep."

For two weeks Mrs. Brown acted as royal stand-in while the jeep was driven round and round Baraza Arena. The driver had thirty-six pages of written instructions to follow.

"What did it feel like to be Princess Margaret?" reporters asked the American woman.

"Rather peculiar," she replied. "I did not know what to do."

The royal visitor benefited from Mrs. Brown's suggestions, for she had found the jeep steps too high for small women. She also said the seat covers were dirty and these had to be changed. Then the jeep jerked when stopping and starting and this too was remedied!

When one thinks how many times a movie scene is made over before the final "take," it's rather amazing that Margaret and other members of her family can carry out their intricate programs so perfectly without a single rehearsal!

During the opening of the three new deep-water berths on the quayside at Dar-Es-Salaam, eager crowds once more got out of hand, but this time Margaret appeared quite unperturbed. She was getting used to such loving demonstrations, frightening though some of them might be.

While in the city she received a poem written in her honor by a Tanga fisherman. It had won him seventy five dollars in a local newspaper contest. Spoken in Swahili, it had to be translated for the Princess whom he had described as the "Star of Freedom." The simple poem read:

> "Our soil is too hard for the seed of revolt
> But fertile for quick growth
> And the spread of good seed."

Before leaving Dar-Es-Salaam, Margaret did some personal shopping. In a tiny Indian store filled with curios she spotted an ebony carving of a water hog and, mistaking it for a pig, said, "I like pigs."

Later she left with her "pig" and some grass mats, while the excited storekeeper proudly declined any payment.

At Tabora hundreds of Wagogo warriors with shining spears and gaily-colored shields staged a mock battle. The Princess became so enthralled with her first glimpse of primitive Africa that she couldn't resist the urge to leave her jeep and mingle freely with forty thousand tribesmen and their women folk. The officials in the royal party were most upset, for they felt that Princess Margaret deliberately took an unnecessary risk. The Africans thought differently, a guard of honor was immediately formed for their "little mother" by tall Gogo warriors armed with broad bladed spears and huge panga knives.

During a trip to Tanga, center of the sisal industry, an old African woman gate-crashed a reception given by the chiefs and, grasping Margaret's gloved hand, shook it heartily and inquired, "How are you, my daughter?"

"Very well, thank you," said the surprised Princess, who didn't mind one bit although the chiefs were peeved by the interruption.

During a native rally at Arusha, Kenya, the Princess came face-to-face with a man she had never met and yet who, but for the hand of fate, might then have been her brother-in-law. It was District Commissioner Francis Townsend, thirty-one, brother of her lost love, Peter Townsend. Without so much as a blush or the blink of an eyelid Margaret greeted him with a brilliant smile and a, "Very pleased to meet you!"

In Kenya one of her bright spots was a drumming exhibition given by two teams, each composing fifty Africans from the Chuka district of the Meru country. The men, dressed in grass skirts with headdresses made

from the white fur of the colobus monkey, swayed backward and forward as they stood astride hollowed tree-
trunk drums. Their eyes were circled with red, white
and blue rings; bracelet beads jangled together, and
each drum beat cracked sharp as a gun.

Princess Margaret was thrilled and asked to meet the
head drummer. "I thought the dancers were wonderful,"
she told him.

At the farm of August Kuenzler, a Swiss big game
hunter, she was invited to select a pair of zebras as a gift.
Eight young animals had been separated into different
pens, but even the sight of a beautiful princess could
not lure them into the open where they could be properly seen.

Margaret ducked under a stockade and visited a baby
giraffe, helped give a young hippopotamus its bottle
and received a baby elephant who had better manners
than the zebras and, of its own accord, came forward to
be unofficially presented. Somehow the Princess managed
to choose her zebras, which have long since been shipped
home to England.

During this tour on one occasion Margaret put common sense before protocol. The heat was suffocating, yet
short evening dresses and dinner jackets had been
banned because somebody gave the word that Margaret
would be wearing a long dress. At the last minute she
walked in on the brilliant clothes-choked assembly wearing a cool short gown—and no gloves.

On leaving Kenya the merry Princess said to the
governor, "See you later, alligator."

There is no record of his reply.

Chapter Twenty-five

COOL, MAN, COOL

It has been suggested that Princess Margaret be known as Princess of the Caribbean. Certainly nobody deserves the title more.

Her latest tour of this part of the world was a triumph. "She's cool, man—real cool," laughed an excited member of the crowd that greeted her in ninety-degree heat at Belize, British Honduras.

While her ladies in waiting seemed hot and bothered, the Princess always looked as if she had just stepped out of an icebox. "How does she do it?" inquired members of the press, wiping perspiring brows.

"It's simple," said Miss Iris Peake, chief lady in waiting. "The Princess simply doesn't feel the heat as we do. In fact, she loves it. She takes no special precautions and wears no special make-up."

For two weeks Margaret had spent at least half the royal program outside in the broiling tropical sunshine —and unlike most of the inhabitants she wore only small hats to protect herself.

Princess Margaret started her tour at Port-of-Spain, Trinidad, arriving with her hair arranged in the new "coconut" coiffure. Beforehand she had confessed to close friends that her wardrobe on this trip would be "rather daring." It certainly was!

"The Dolly Princess," even wore her own version of the "sack"—a loose-belted, sleeveless creation in silk designed by Victor Stiebel. Although it hid her tiny waist, the Princess didn't mind. She found it ideally suited to the hot weather. Then, stepping out one day at Port-of-Spain, she wore a bright puffed skirt with harem hemline. This she complemented with a wide-brimmed sailor hat and peek-toe shoes.

Margaret had a field day with hats in the West Indies. One by Simone Mirman made of white organdie was shaped like a milkmaid's bonnet and decorated with outsize hatpins.

Margaret's visit was an official state one to mark the official opening on April 22 of the new West Indies Legislature. In three weeks she covered more than eleven thousand miles, visiting not only the Federation's islands but British Honduras and British Guiana as well. Her job was to bring a foundation of unity to the far-flung isles.

Acting for her sovereign sister, the Princess inaugurated the Federation's first parliament. This put into effect the new constitution that links the following Caribbean islands: Antigua, Barbados, Dominica,

Grenada, Jamaica, Montserrat, Trinidad and Tobago, St. Lucia, St. Vincent and St. Kitts-Nevis.

Margaret looked most regal in her long white ceremonial gown and glittering diamonds as she sat on the speaker's throne of the Legislative Council Chamber. She told the newly-elected members of the House of Representatives that they had "the great responsibility of insuring that the Federation grows in strength and purpose."

Margaret's tour was at all times filled with colorful incidents but none more amusing than the tale of fifty men on a hot tin roof.

The Princess was all set to officiate in the solemn stone-laying ceremony at a West Indian town hall. Fanfares of trumpets sounded, the crowd waited in silent expectation, and then—CRASH—there was a roar like the beating of a hundred drums as the rusted tin of a hot roof suddenly collapsed, and with it the men who were standing on top. Twenty of them slid noisily into the middle of a hundred bicycles stored underneath. The crowd burst into laughter—and so did the Princess. Only one man was hurt, and he broke his leg. This was no tragedy for to his delight he immediately became the local celebrity and will probably make good subject material for the Calypso men to sing about.

A great welcome was awaiting Margaret as she sailed into Georgetown on the *Canje Pheasant*. She had sailed twenty miles up the brown waters of the Demerara River to the capital of British Guiana, her ship surrounded by small craft all decorated with Union Jacks and red, white and blue bunting.

It was all rather ironic, the cheering, the waving and the hand-clapping. The arrival was one of the most spontaneous demonstrations of good will during the entire trip, although the leader of the local political party in power, the People's Progressive Party, Dr. Cheddi Jagan, is pro-Communist and anti-royalist.

Jagan, a dentist by occupation, and his Chicago-born wife, described by the British press as "Red Janet," master-minded a plot four years ago to set up a Communist-dominated state in British Guiana. That was before British troops moved in.

"We do not want to be a colony shackled to Britain, but a dominion with internal self-government," Dr. Jagan told reporters. "I shall welcome the Princess not as a political figure but as a national figurehead."

He bowed slightly as he shook Margaret's hand. "Red Janet" made neither curtsey or bow.

Toward the end of the tour four jet bombers raced over the Atlantic to protect the Princess on her arrival in British Honduras. Secret Service agents had warned the British Government that the anti-British Guatemalan Government planned to send planes over Belize, capital of British Honduras on the South American mainland to demonstrate against the royal visit. The Prime Minister, Harold Macmillan, decided to send four Canberras when the Secret Service further reported that Guatemalan pilots planned to "scream" over the house tops as Margaret passed through the streets.

The presence of the Canberras was effective and there was no unpleasantness. The "Dolly Princess" carried out all her engagements without a hitch.

Chapter Twenty-six

WHY MARGARET SAW TOWNSEND AGAIN

Princess Margaret, determined to save Peter Townsend from a life sentence of self-imposed exile abroad, purposely saw her rejected lover again.

The tea party at Clarence House on March 26, 1958, was a very proper and pleasant affair. By receiving Peter at Clarence House in the presence of her mother—who, like her father, once thought of the handsome flier as the son they never had—she has shown there is no hard feeling between the royal family and Townsend. Elizabeth and Philip were in Holland visiting Queen Juliana—an absence that was noted by observers around the world. Group Captain Townsend had arrived from Brussels earlier that afternoon, and at four o'clock presented himself at the Princess's London home.

It was on October 19, 1955, that they had kept their last tryst at Uckfield House, Sussex, England. Since then Townsend had made a lonely sixty-thousand-mile journey to far parts of the world. Although in such places as Japan he was mobbed by bobby-soxers, back home in his native Britain the man who had aspired to marry the Queen's only sister had become the forgotten man.

Like the Duke of Windsor, Townsend, it seemed, was to be faced with a bleak future abroad. In England he was only an embarrassment. In contrast, by her sacrifice for religious reasons and duty to the British Commonwealth, Princess Margaret had grown more dear than ever to British hearts. However, a great lover of children, recently dubbed "the Children's Princess" by a British provincial newspaper, she had also been disturbed by knowing all the time that Townsend felt himself unwelcome in England while his two young sons, Giles and Hugo George, were being deprived of a father's love and guidance at the age when they most needed it.

Because of the present shortage of royal relatives, she performs lone duties never before entrusted to a spinster princess. She has been described as "the brightest jewel in Elizabeth's crown" and as an ambassador of good will has represented her sister on royal tours around the world.

Although Britishers were apparently taken by surprise at the meeting, others living on the continent of Europe were not. That the meeting would take place had been rumored for many weeks in France and Belgium where Townsend has many close friends.

Queen Elizabeth and Prince Philip were not surprised either, although there were complaints from some court officials that Margaret's reunion with Peter had wiped her sister's successful Dutch visit off the front pages. Margaret had told Elizabeth of the coming meeting before the Queen left the country. She insisted on her right to see her own friends, and Elizabeth saw no reason why she should not.

Townsend, bronzed and forty-three, looked happy when he left Clarence House at six fifty in the evening. The Princess was radiant and smiling when she later attended a play at the Carlton Theater.

Speculation snowballed again. Had Margaret resorted to a woman's prerogative and changed her mind? The answer was NO, and through his lawyer, Alan Phillpotts, Townsend issued the following statement: "There are no grounds whatever for supposing that my seeing Princess Margaret in any way alters the situation declared specifically in the Princess' statement in the autumn of 1955."

However, Margaret has gone on having Peter Townsend in for "tea and sympathy" and on May 21, 1958, Queen Elizabeth herself gave explicit instructions for an official clearing of the air. That morning a report on Margaret and Townsend had appeared in the Swiss newspaper *Tribune de Geneve*.

The statement from Buckingham Palace read: "The press secretary to the Queen is authorized to say that the report in the *Tribune de Geneve* concerning a possible engagement between Princess Margaret and Group Captain Peter Townsend is entirely untrue. Her Royal Highness' statement of 1955 remains unaltered."

Such a denial from the palace which seldom, if ever, takes notice of rumor was in itself most unusual.

Chapter Twenty-seven

MARGARET IN WONDERLAND

" And about time too," declared Princess Margaret when her plans to visit Canada were finally approved. She had often complained at being the only adult member of her immediate family who hadn't visited that dominion.

Announcing details of her tour, the Prime Minister of Canada, the Right Honorable John G. Diefenbaker said: "In planning the journey, we endeavored to provide ample opportunity for Her Royal Highness to meet informally as many Canadians as possible and to enjoy the Canadian summer." However, three provinces found themselves left out of the royal itinerary and were very upset—Manitoba with its key city of Winnipeg (a rising center for the arts), Newfoundland and Prince Edward Island.

Also, the people of the United States, who have always been extremely partial to the democratic Margaret, were to be disappointed. President Eisenhower, knowing of the princess' desire to visit his country, had tactfully suggested to Elizabeth when she was his guest at the White House that "it would be nice if your sister could come to Washington next summer while she is in Canada."

The Queen was delighted, Margaret was overjoyed, but the British Foreign Office said, "No."

It was considered that a visit by Margaret so soon after her sister's successful good-will trip to the United States would serve no useful purpose.

Her most important official duty on her Canadian calendar was her presence at the centennial of British Columbia.

For days before leaving London Margaret's Scottish maid Ruby was busy packing the new collection of gowns and hats that were in turn to delight and shock Canadians. During her stay she was to do more to popularize the trapeze-style dress than a score of movie stars.

Just before her departure Queen Elizabeth became ill with acute sinusitis and overwork. The Queen Mother immediately took her place at an important Buckingham Palace garden party and was assisted by Princess Margaret. It was a great success and Margaret made it her business to seek out a number of the many Canadians present, for she was eager to discuss her coming tour.

Guests wandered through the palace gardens, peeped through a window at the model of a hand-painted galleon whose owner, Prince Charles, was away at school, and were delighted to find the cushions on the garden furniture soiled from use like any other family's.

The Queen Mother especially enjoyed the music from the Broadway hit, *My Fair Lady,* which the orchestra was playing. Dressed in pale apricot organza, she gaily tapped time with her finger to the tune of "With a Little Bit of Luck."

By her side was the little Duchess of Gloucester (Margaret's Aunt Alice) who had her right arm in a black sling. However, this did not prevent her from shaking the hand of every guest with her index finger, including 250 debutantes from all parts of the British Commonwealth.

The Queen Mother drove to the London Airport to see Princess Margaret off. Margaret had been particularly concerned about her Sealyham terriers, Johnny and Pipkin, and the Queen Mother promised to exercise them regularly.

The journey to Vancouver, British Columbia was made by a long-range, turbo-prop Britannia airliner flying the Polar curve route.

Along with Margaret went two ladies in waiting, a private secretary, a doctor, an airman (not Group-Captain Townsend but Group-Captain A. D. Mitchell, deputy captain of the Queen's flight, who supervises all her air travel), a press officer, a clerk comptroller, a woman secretary, a detective, two dressers, two footmen, two maids to the ladies in waiting, and M. René Moulard, her famed hairdresser. Margaret also took one hundred pieces of air-weight luggage.

The menu department of British Overseas Airways

had done a wonderful job of facing the catering problem for the long nineteen-hour journey which "loses time" all the way to Vancouver. At all times they had snacks on hand including Margaret's favorite strawberries in port wine.

Excited as a teenager, the girl who was to be tagged "a living doll" the moment she touched down in Canada, took out her cine-camera and started making more home movies to aid Princess Anne's geography lessons back in the Palace. With much enthusiasm she "fired away" at the snow-capped Rockies down below.

Margaret changed planes at Vancouver where the newspapers had complained she would have to be like Alice in Wonderland and pretend not to be seen. As an air force spokesman said: "Our instructions were to conduct ourselves as if the Princess were invisible." The plane in which she flew from England was too large to land at Victoria, British Columbia, her final destination, and since protocol demanded that the first official greeting come from the representative of the Canadian Government, Defense Minister George Pearkes, in Victoria, nobody else could greet her at her change-over landing in Victoria.

As one airman said, "How does an AC2 reply respectfully to an invisible princess?"

In London they called it "the time to smile, but not to stay."

Invisible she might officially be, but Margaret waved gaily to the hundreds of sun-tanned faces that had gathered at the airport—and hoped they could see her.

In preparation for her landing at Victoria the Royal

Canadian Mounted Police had taken many security precautions. They were afraid that the unpredictable "Duk-
hobor Freedomites" might stage one of their undressing
or bombing demonstrations on the way to her hotel.
As for the undressing, they couldn't have known that
when Margaret's favorite Aunt Marina had been receiving chiefs in far-off Malaya one turned up without any
trousers but the Duchess didn't turn a hair!

The Dukhobors, meaning "spirit wrestlers," are members of a Russian religious sect founded in the early part
of the eighteenth century. They refuse to recognize any
temporal authority, insisting that all men are equal and
children of God. After being persecuted by the Czarist
authorities in the nineteenth century, many of them
emigrated to Canada while others settled in Mexico.

Being informed of Princess Margaret's habit of elud
ing the police and wandering off on her own, the police
were a little jittery during her pleasant stay in British
Columbia.

Victoria's church bells and a twenty-one gun salute
welcomed the Princess when she landed. Margaret, who
was wearing a pale blue trapeze-style gown that confused
male news commentators describing the scene ("Is it a
sack or a trapeze?"), immediately drove to the royal suite
at the Empress Hotel.

There Margaret must have felt she was visiting some
old Sussex manor house. Pseudo-Tudor paneling, a large
fireplace with an artificial grate, and dark oak floors gave
off an air of solid respectability. The furniture smelled
of wax, for the British Columbians, as the British themselves, take a great pride in polishing their furniture.

A large oak refectory table flanked by a group of dig-nified-looking chairs contrasted with the white tile and stainless steel of an adjoining butler's pantry.

Hidden in a corner of Margaret's sitting room was a television set and there was a generous sprinkling of cut-glass ash trays for the first of Britain's female royalty to smoke in public.

Margaret's bedroom windows opened above a curving lily pond alive with pink and white blossoms. Overhang-ing the pool was an arbutus with rose-colored trunk.

Flower beds filled with blue, purple and pink hydran-geas and soft green lawns stretched down toward the harbor, bright with its gaily painted yachts.

By her bed the princess placed the favorite photograph of Peter Townsend which she never travels without, and a few hours after her arrival he telephoned her. They spoke for half an hour while Canadians talked openly of the "royal romance."

She also found a letter waiting for her from the flyer, written of course before she left England. Her eagerness to stay at Kelowna on Okanagan Lake for several days was said to be because Townsend had told her it was one of the most beautiful places he had visited in Canada.

Just inside the door of her suite was placed a bronze of Diamond Jubilee, once a winner of England's famed Derby. It was one of a number of pieces left in the suite by Lieutenant Governor Frank M. Ross and Mrs. Ross, knowing of Margaret's love of horses, to make the prin-cess feel more at home. They vacated the royal suite for her stay.

When Government House burned down the bronze

horse was one of the few treasures to be saved. It fell through the floor into the basement where firemen rescued it. The statue had been left to the governor many years before by a friend in England.

One of Margaret's first inquiries was, "Where is there some good swimming?" She was lucky, for in addition to all the out-of-door places to swim the Empress has the Crystal Garden, Canada's largest glass-covered pool.

All of "oh-so-British" Victoria was happy, even if some of the more sedate of the residents were a little worried that the princess would be mobbed by "those dreadful tourists" wearing shorts. An editorial in Toronto's *Telegram* summed it all up with the words, "British Columbians like the real-life Princess. They are impressed by the clear dedication to the job she has to do. And amused by the merry twinkle that sometimes mildly shocks people: a bare-armed dress to church and, afterwards, a gin and tonic."

A later editorial in the same newspaper declared with obvious sincerity, "This gay child, who was rightly called the Sweetheart of the Commonwealth, has grown into womanhood without losing the charm of her youth, yet in maturity has added an obvious sense of responsibility to balance her love of fun and frolic. She has inherited from her mother the title of Britain's finest ambassador."

On her first Sunday morning in Canada Princess Margaret attended Christ Church Cathedral. She was a little late, having paused on the way to accept a bouquet from a child. There were 1,500 fortunate ticket-holders for seats in the cathedral but even they had been standing in line long before the doors were opened an hour before.

It was a happy coincidence, and one that brought her close to the memory of her beloved father, George VI, that she was to sit close to the wrought-iron altar rail before which her parents were married, April 26, 1923. It had been a gift to the cathedral from Westminster Abbey.

The tapestry that hung so proudly behind the altar itself was used in the royal robing room at the coronation of her sister. Tiny golden crowns and Tudor roses were embroidered on a rich blue ground. The Bishop's Chair, blitzed during the Battle of Britain, came from St. Paul's Cathedral.

It was a glittering scene with a touch of bright color provided by the scarlet uniform of the Mounted Police inspector who watched the princess all through the service. Margaret herself wore a simple, pale blue silk sack gown and a funny little yellow hat with a bright artificial daisy bobbing up and down in front.

Stan Cole, the verger, had diligently searched through the hymn books to find one that looked new for her. Before the service he confessed to having given the pew in which she was to sit "one last polish." He also re-arranged the vases of lilies whose strong scent drifted down to the congregation.

The service was conducted by Dean Brian Whitlow who didn't change its form from that used any other Sunday.

"This is the service," he declared, "that has been said in this church for 104 years. It is the familiar service the Princess has known for twenty-seven years. It is just a coincidence that they have come together here."

The Dean's sermon was clearly not addressed personally to the princess, who never misses a service at home, when he derided those people who thought that finding God "in romantic sounding places like the forest and on the golf courses" was as good as going to church. "Stay away from church and chill your own souls," he warned.

Princess Margaret took out a two dollar and a one dollar bill from her handbag for the collection. It is not usual for her to carry money except on such occasions. The money was roughly the equivalent of a pound in British currency, a generous offering for a Sunday service.

During the afternoon the Princess made a private call on behalf of her mother. It was to the large ranch belonging to Mrs. William (Ruth) Woodward, widow of a former Lieutenant Governor of British Columbia. The Woodwards had been hosts to Margaret's parents when they toured Canada in 1939. Four happy hours were spent on the ranch and beach. After tea she returned somewhat sunburned to her suite at the Empress Hotel.

At her special request and in a way reminiscent of her brother-in-law Prince Philip, Margaret arranged to meet the press.

A large crowd said to number 1,860 turned up and respected her request not to bring their cameras. A sofa, two chairs and a table had been set up for the princess but when she arrived for what must be one of the biggest cocktail parties on record, she completely ignored the sofa. Then, lighting a cigarette which she held in an extra long black and gold holder, she strolled among her guests.

She looked very much the woman of the world that

evening with her bouffant hair-do and a faint trace of mascara about her clear blue eyes. One man gallantly tried to light her cigarette but, after several unsuccessful attempts to find his lighter while Margaret waited, at last resorted to a good old fashioned match. Young men collected Margaret's cigarette butts for souvenirs while she did most of the talking, stopping every so often for a sip at her whisky and soda.

In an interview Margaret gives the feeling that she is always one jump ahead of you, anticipating in advance what you are going to say. Bette Davis, the American actress, gives the same impression. They are both small women, sweet on the surface, but far from demure underneath and very outspoken.

To the crew of the *Toronto Telegram Weekend Magazine* who had been with her on the recent Caribbean tour and whom she immediately recognized, Margaret said, "Everyone enjoyed themselves, the crowds, the entertainers. Everything was so spontaneous. It was such fun."

She also had quite a lot to say about dress.

When told that she looked nice in the "sack" she quipped, "Yes, but being rather short I naturally can't wear the chemise. You see," she laughed, "I must have my waistline marked, at least in the front."

"But you are wearing your skirts shorter!"

"Yes, between fifteen and sixteen inches. Today's dress is sixteen inches. Yesterday's was fifteen."

She confessed to liking the dress designs of Victor Steibel of London very much because "his clothes are always new-looking but pretty."

"I do not think that the London couturiers will continue the sack or the chemise particularly, this fall," she prophesied. "But certainly they will the trapeze."

To this somebody whispered, "She's doing everything to see that they do."

For royal tours in hot weather the new loose-fitting garment must be a gift from heaven.

During her "meet the press" interlude she also dropped the hint that she considered the gift of seventy gallons of drinking water a right royal one. It had been filtered three times and especially purified to protect her from stomach upsets due to daily changes in drinking water. On other royal tours Margaret has suffered with severe stomach upsets and the sympathetic British Columbians were taking no chances.

The water originally came from Vancouver's municipal supply. After being treated with chemicals it was put into large bottles bearing royal purple labels complete with coronets and the inscription, "Table water. In honor of the visit of Her Royal Highness Princess Margaret."

She was also amused to learn that her portrait sporting the latest hair-do had made its appearance on a special set of table dishes.

By using the tradesmen's entrance, Princess Margaret managed to slip quietly away to see a few of the local beauty spots without interference of crowds or fuss.

She did the parks and shore in a car chauffeured by a mounty, driving past the tallest totem pole in the world, which she photographed, and on toward the distant mountains.

Wearing an angora wool sweater and a head-scarf, Margaret never missed a thing. She admired the roses with which the gardens abound, surprised a group of tourists on the mountain top who were too startled to cheer, and waved approvingly at an old lady who was patiently walking a dog.

Margaret being the chief topic of conversation in Victoria, some of the visitors' and residents' comments are interesting.

Said London's *Daily Mail* representative on the day of her arrival, "She is very religious, you know. She will probably go off for private prayers even before church tomorrow."

"More likely to find herself a piano," said the *News of the World* man.

One irate elderly lady, peeved because the Princess had not appeared on the hotel balcony to be viewed just two minutes after arrival, snapped: "I think it's disgraceful. It's the government's fault. In England they would always come out for a minute or two."

"She's just finished a long and tiring journey," said another woman more sympathetically, to which her little boy added, "She might want to go to the bathroom."

"Well, she doesn't have to unpack and go through customs," sniffed the first woman. "I do, when I travel."

Mrs. Walter Ihle of Chico, California, accompanied by her husband and four-year-old son, Billy, was another lady with a point of view. "We think royalty is fine," she declared. "Some English people seem to have misgivings because of the cost, but not us. She's a princess. She's a good scout."

"We want Margaret. We want Margaret," yelled Dr. Everett Johnson, an evangelist from Sacramento, California. When more than half an hour after her arrival he learned the royal suite was in the north wing of the hotel, not near the main entrance, he led the eager crowd to the north driveway.

In one ceremony a lady protested loudly because her view of the Princess was obstructed by a hefty mounty. Pocket-sized Margaret heard the complaint and in a gesture that would have done justice to Grannie England, tapped him smartly on the shoulder and asked very sweetly if he would kindly get out of the way.

Two young Americans, Mr. and Mrs. Robert Keith of Whidbey Island, Washington, flew their own airplane to Victoria for the royal weekend.

Said Mrs. Keith, "This is sort of unreal, but very nice. It arouses something fine in the people."

"Royalty is very necessary," Mr. Keith chimed in. "It adds a great deal to the morale and spirit of the people. We can maybe see the value of this more objectively than you can. It is the realization of everybody's dreams."

Of Margaret's Navy honor-guard, bystander David Christian had this to say: "I think the navy is in perfect precision—just about as perfect as you can get. Princess Margaret should have been here before, since Canada is one of the major countries in the Commonwealth."

There was nostalgia too among some elderly Canadians, many who had emigrated from Europe.

Some of these were reminded of other royal personages, now only names in the history books.

"Best ceremony I've ever seen," said Michael Marjanovich, seventy-two, who was born in Serbia, now part of Yugoslavia. He was talking to David Francis of Victoria's *Daily Colonist* and he had tears in his eyes. "I never felt so bad as now."

Then the old gentleman recalled his own royal memories of a boyhood spent in Serbia under the rule of King Alexander and Queen Draga. "He was like anybody else," he said. "I have seen him hundreds of times. The King and Queen often came in the school to visit." The royal couple were assassinated in 1903. "Today," he complained, "Yugoslavia is a Communist state ruled by Marshal Tito, and King Peter is in exile in France."

Michael leaned heavily on his cane and proudly fingered a button he always carries to indicate he worked in munitions during both world wars. "The Communists take everything, no matter what you've got," he declared. "You've got to do what the Communists want."

Mrs. Jan Selsing, now a resident of Victoria, also recalled another royal family. She had her six-year-old son Mickey, resplendent in a miniature Royal Canadian Mounted Police uniform, with her. With her forester husband she came from Copenhagen, Denmark just six years ago. "The last day before we left for Canada we met the Danish Queen Ingrid and the three princesses. Nobody paid any attention to them. They were just walking in the street.

"The Danish Royal Family has much less protocol surrounding it than your own. Of course, if you meet them officially, you curtsy."

She then recalled that when the late King Frederik IX moved to a castle outside Copenhagen the children, including herself, used to take him posies of wildflowers. "Sometimes he would sit the children on his horse in front of him," she remembered with a smile. "During the Second World War he made a practice of riding through Copenhagen on his horse."

Mrs. Selsing's nine-year-old daughter, Jette, was among the Brownies who greeted the former Brownie of Buckingham Palace. So was Roslyn, daughter of Mrs. Bert Johns.

"This is really something for the children to see," declared the enthusiastic Mrs. Johns. "My parents were English and you have to hold up for the Royal Family. We have so little to hold and respect these days."

She was delighted that her daughter, along with the other Brownies, had a good view of the Princess "instead of being shoved into the background."

"When Queen Elizabeth, then a princess, and her husband visited here, Roslyn slept through it all," Mrs. Johns recalled. "I am awfully anxious to see Princess Margaret," she continued, "for she is such a controversial figure."

Margaret was good for the airlines. During the first weekend an all-time record number of bookings from Vancouver to Victoria was recorded by officials. Trans-Canada Air Lines brought big North Star airliners into service on the run to cope wtih 7,200 passengers going to Vancouver Island for a glimpse of the star attraction. The company had to put seventy-five extra passenger agents on its staff, and handled more than twenty thousand phone calls daily.

At Margaret's request, movies of her first two days in British Columbia were shown on television at a certain time so that she could be at hand to watch them in the privacy of her suite. She is always critical of her own appearance and wanted to see how her wardrobe looked on the screen.

"The word 'chemise' is taboo this fall," the fashion papers said.

"New York designers are ready to lift the curtain on fall collections which take many and varied shapes, all influenced by the chemise but called by other names— the unfitted silhouette, the relaxed sheath, the easy look or the liberty line.

"The new shapes of fashion are diverse, but they have several points in common. All hang loosely on the body, all reveal the knees and all avoid recognition of the natural waistline.

"By far the predominant silhouette for fall is the high-waisted Empire line, known variously as the camise, the Directoire look and the Josephine theme."

The princess noted the last with some satisfaction, for hadn't her own Empress Josephine hair style created by René for the first West Indian Tour caused a ripple among hair-conscious women throughout the world?

Margaret was especially delighted to receive an illuminated address and fealty together with a specially bound replica of the first issue of *The Colonist*, Victoria's newspaper, bearing the date December 11, 1858. A hundred years later the newspaper is still flourishing and in a special presentation number of its weekly magazine supplement, "The Islander," published in honor of

the Princess's visit and edited by John Shaw, was included a chapter of the biography you are reading.

In an editorial *The Daily Colonist* said, "It has been
the historical lot of the port of Victoria to be linked
closely with the Motherland of the British Commonwealth. For many of its earliest years it drew sustenance
and guidance directly through the aegis of the Crown
the Princess Margaret so ably represents. Her Royal
Highness will not be unmindful of the fact that her
gracious forebear, Queen Victoria, gave her name to this
city, nor of the loyalty expressed in two great world con-
flicts by the sons and daughters of this community. To
the physical ties that past and present have bound Victoria to the royal house there is in addition the personal
attachment which today is appreciated more than ever."

Queen Victoria's statue stands in front of the Legislature near Margaret's hotel. In fact there were times
when it seemed the great queen was actually pointing
her scepter at her great-great-granddaughter.

What would Victoria, the woman whose name sets a
seal of propriety and modesty, have thought of this descendant of hers? Would she have been shocked?

Personally, I don't think so. Victoria was a part of the
times in which she lived, when it wasn't thought proper
even to show a bare ankle. Like Queen Mary, whom she
admired so much ("Thank God!" she wrote in her diary,
"Georgie has got such an excellent, useful and good
wife"), Victoria would have moved with the times.

Would she have approved of the Townsend romance?
Well, she did say, "Those who go to the divorce courts
cannot come to mine," but she was just as determined as

Margaret on the subject of loving. When her beloved Albert died she ran like a mad thing through the lonely corridors of Windsor Castle, her screams terrible to hear. The queen who was so much a queen was in her weakness very much a woman, going into a period of mourning from which she never wholly emerged. This might have seemed selfish to those who did not know the depth of her unreasoning love. Like Margaret with Townsend's picture which travels everywhere with her, Victoria would receive her prime minister with a bust of Albert on the table beside her, a wreath of flowers hung around the white marble throat. She was determined never to be allowed to forget him even for a minute. In her bedroom at Windsor was hung a picture of herself dressed like a nun with Albert hovering as a ghostly visitant in the background; she placed another portrait wreathed with *immortelles* over the empty pillow beside her.

In Victoria, British Columbia, Margaret noticed that Victoria's statue was complete with wedding ring, which reminded her of a family story. Somebody once made the remark in jest that the famed statue of Queen Victoria standing in the Mall to the front of Buckingham Palace was minus such a symbol of marriage. It had not been meant for Queen Mary's ears but she overheard and later, when she thought nobody was looking, sent a trusted servant to see if the remark were true. It was, but Queen Mary soon made it her business to ensure that Victoria's statue had a fine new wedding ring sculptured onto her plump finger!

If Victoria showed devotion, individuality, and

strength of character in the habit of loving, so did certain members on the maternal side of Margaret's ancestry, the Lyons of Glamis. King Robert II of Scotland, a gay blade if ever there was one, is said to have had such a multitude of children of both sexes when he was young that he had to obtain a special dispensation from the Pope before he could marry respectably.

Then there was Lady Janet Douglas, wife of the sixth Lord Glamis, who in 1537 was charged with "conspiring the King's death by poison." Although she was condemned to death and burned at the stake, the charge was later found to be a pure invention.

During the opening days of her tour two things were to bring concern to Princess Margaret. First, her sister's illness. Elizabeth was more sick than the official bulletins led one to believe. Her nasal condition was so painful that X-rays were necessary.

Then there was the crisis in the Middle East over Lebanon, Iraq and Jordan. The murder of the twenty-two-year-old King Feisal II of Iraq was particularly painful to her, for he was a frequent visitor to Britain where his family have a pleasant country home, Stanwell Place, near Staines, Middlesex. His beautiful fiancée, Princess Fazilet, seventeen, was studying in Heathfield School, Ascot, England, at the time of his death. The former Harrow schoolboy's smiling face was well known in the British press. Margaret remembered the happy visit he had with Elizabeth, Philip, the Queen Mother and herself. It did not seem possible that he had died so violently.

There is a saying that when one hears of a death a

birth is soon to follow. In Canada there were many births during the royal visit and, in the case of girls, Margaret of course was the most popular name given to the new arrivals.

Margaret carried out the primary duty on her visit to British Columbia with such dignity that nobody could possibly complain. The history of this most British of provinces is an interesting one. Captain Cook explored a part of the coast of British Columbia in 1787, and a settlement was made by the English ten years later at Nootka. However, the settlement was broken up by the Spanish who claimed the coast as far north as latitude 61°, where the territory of Russia was supposed to end.

In 1846 the question of possession was settled by diplomacy, when the United States relinquished its claim and the territory now in British Columbia became a possession of the British Crown.

The claims of the United States were based on the Louisiana Purchase and explorations made by Lewis and Clark. Out of these claims grew the campaign cry of "Fifty-four forty or fight," at the time Polk was elected President of the U.S.

Vancouver Island was organized as a crown colony as early as 1849, but little progress was made in developing the country until the discovery of gold in 1858, when settlers began to pour into British Columbia, and it was made a crown colony the same year. The two colonies were united in 1866 under the name of British Columbia.

In 1873 a dispute in regard to the boundary was sub-

mitted to the Emperor of Germany, who awarded the
San Juan Islands to the U.S. The colony entered the
Dominion in 1871, under an agreement that the federal
government should provide railway connection with the
Atlantic coast, and this was accomplished in 1887, when
the Canadian Pacific Railway was opened for traffic.

Unlike most of us, Princess Margaret woke up ready
for work on Monday morning. The heading in the list
of official arrangements read: Monday, July 14. Dress:
Formal.

Accompanied by the Honorable Frank M. Ross, Lieutenant-Governor of British Columbia, she was met at the
steps of City Hall by Mayor P. B. Scurrah. A dais had
been erected in front of the freshly painted building and
there the princess met the reeves of neighboring munic-
ipalities. After signing the visitors' book she was given
the special gold coin minted to celebrate the centennial.

Then in a motor cavalcade she drove to the parliament
buildings and gazed up to where the newly gilded figure
of Captain George Vancouver topped the dome. It looks
out across the harbor into which he sailed in April, 1791.

This visit to the parliament buildings symbolized the
purpose of Margaret's trip to the province and there she
took part in various ceremonies of an official nature,
meeting dignitaries and their wives, inspecting a guard
of honor, and hearing an address of welcome from Premier W. A. C. Bennett.

Princess Margaret, like Robinson Crusoe, suddenly
found herself the proud owner of an island—Portland
Island, one of the Gulf Island group in the Morseby

Passage, six miles northeast of Sidney. To a girl who has received everything on her travels from a live zebra to an African chief's supper tray, gifts do not always come as a surprise, but British Columbia's island was probably the biggest she's ever received. It also turned out to be somewhat embarrassing, as an Indian chief declared the British Columbia government didn't own the land it gave to Margaret. He even went so far as to ask Prime Minister Diefenbaker to advise her not to accept it.

Chief Andy Paull, president of the North American Indian Brotherhood, said in an open letter to the prime minister that acceptance of the gift by Princess Margaret "would not be in keeping with the dignity and solemnity of Her Highness, in that the B. C. Government does not own any of the islands in B. C.—nor do they own all that now is known as British Columbia."

Recreation Minister Earle C. Westwood had stated that on Margaret's acceptance the island would be developed as a provincial marine park.

Chief Paull went even further and said that the government couldn't make the gift because the land was guaranteed to the Indians under the British North America Act.

"The B. C. government has persistently refused to comply with the proclamation of King George III in 1763. . . ." he declared, "wherein His Majesty proclaimed that the native Indians must be compensated for their lands and that they should meet the Indians in council for the extinguishment of the native title—and this has never been done." The Chief also said that another decree made in 1858 by Queen Victoria had promised compensation to the Indians.

Margaret did accept the 540-acre island, once the private retreat of General Francis (One-Arm) Sutton, eccentric millionaire and soldier of fortune who served as military leader to a Chinese warlord.

Six sterling silver spoons were missing after Victoria's royal garden party given by the Lieutenant-Governor in the Government House gardens. A crowd of 4,500 persons attended the social event of the year—the men in starched shirt fronts—in ninety-degree heat.

Margaret, looking cool and as erect as one of her sister's guardsmen, stood in a rustic teahouse and nibbled turkey sandwiches while tightly packed guests craned their necks to get a better look at her.

Among the throng Margaret met David Livingstone McKeand, eighty, appropriately named for the famed missionary-explorer, and for many years government representative in the Arctic archipelago. He told Margaret, "I was on the Nascopi. It went down off Cape Dorset in 1946." A member of the first Canadian contingent to the Boer War in 1899, he continued, "I was reviewed by your great-great-grandmother, Victoria, by Edward the Seventh and Eighth, by the Georges, by your sister and now I'm meeting you." Then he added a postscript: "And you're the prettiest of the lot!"

For an official luncheon she appeared in a white sleeveless harem skirt printed with blue cornflowers which was rather startling. The men didn't like it.

Commander D. Bruce Smith, to whose home Margaret

planned to go as a guest at Kelowna, was there talking of plans made for her four-day visit. "We didn't do any special painting-up for her," he confessed. "The Lieutenant-Governor takes over. My wife won't have to do any of the cooking or the work, but she'll have to tell everybody else what to do and where things are." He had also bought a stock of the latest records, including Margaret's favorite "Purple People Eater."

If the menfolks hadn't liked the harem touch they went all out for Margaret's first evening gown of the tour. She wore it to dinner at the Canadian Tourist Club. Of white taffeta printed with red roses and jade green leaves, it was cut low, with off-the-shoulder sleeves.

With Victoria, the capital, at her feet, Princess Margaret left for Nanaimo and the biggest birthday cake in the world. The one the late Mike Todd had made for Elizabeth Taylor at Madison Square Garden did not compare with it.

Twenty feet square at the base, seventeen feet high, weighing ten thousand pounds, it had one hundred glittering candles to symbolize the centenary. Margaret was asked to blow out only one of them and then to cut the first giant slice. She borrowed the Lieutenant-Governor's sword for the job.

The cake had been baked by Mike Farana, a hospital chef, who was allowed a week's leave of absence from his job to complete the task. Under twenty-four-hour guard in readiness for the cutting ceremony, it had five tiers with reproductions of local historical scenes worked into the sides. On top was a crown made of golden candy—in front a sugar-icing replica, three foot long, of the Parliament buildings in Victoria.

Another of Margaret's jobs was to spend some time with a group of Brownies who were disappointed because they had only caught a blurred glimpse of her as the royal car sped by. She heard how they felt and insisted things be put right.

It was like Princess Margaret to want to see the last frontier country in British Columbia's interior. In an RCAF plane she flew the seven hundred miles over mountain and muskeg, movie-camera in hand. How she loves that camera! Maybe one day she will be allowed to publish a book of her photographs for some worthy charity as her great-grandmother, the beautiful Queen Alexandra, did in the early days of photography.

At last she touched down in the fabled Cariboo, which is enjoying greater prosperity today than at any time since the booming days of the great gold rush. Oil, gas and farming are the reasons.

The Brownies and Girl Guides were not as composed as their sisters in Victoria. At Fort St. John they shrieked with delight. The local pipe band composed of six men was on hand to play the Royal Forty-Second March as Margaret entered this energetic little municipality on the Alaska Highway with its population of three thousand plus their 3,600 cars. It was a blazing hot day.

Every bar in town was closed at the suggestion of the renowned "Ma" Margaret Murray, better known as "Meg," editor of the *Alaska Highway News*. Nothing can crush or dampen Ma Murray's courage. Once bombed out of Shanghai, she now writes editorials for her newspaper that keep the local citizenry on their toes and get quoted in other publications across the nation.

Ma told the men who wanted a drink of something stronger than water to buy what they needed and carry it home. "There'll be no beverage rooms open while Princess Margaret is here," she declared. Knowing Ma, the men took her at her word.

Ma made news recently when she advised her neighbors not to flush their toilets more than once a day. Water was at a minimum due to the three-months-long period of drought the area was suffering.

For Margaret's visit Ma turned up in a dress of pink lace, a Coronation medal and—in spite of the heat—a fur boa.

She might have tried to save water on the toilets but where Princess Margaret was concerned it was another matter. "Water shortage or not," said Ma, "we gave the old town a darn good soaking for the Princess. We didn't want the dust to get in her eyes. We sprayed the streets and washed the cars and washed our faces too. We figured it was the least we could do." In fact they used fifty thousand gallons of water.

Police cars with loudspeakers cruised through the town all the previous day asking the people not to drive their cars on the roads, in an effort to stop the choking dust. Just the same there were quite a few thick yellow dust-clouds, but dust has never stopped Margaret yet. She and her mother in Africa once refused to pull their car shades in order to ensure the crowds a better view—and it was very dusty there.

Margaret was driven out to see Pacific Fort St. John Number Four natural gas well and although they had got a nice new orange and black tin safety helmet all ready right down to her name painted on the front she refused point-blank to wear it. Instead, she clung to her petal cloche hat.

A hundred-foot jet of flaming steam shot upward into the blazing afternoon sky and Margaret gasped but didn't move an inch. The heat brought color to her face and she had to shout to be heard over the screeching. Then she went by car to look over a gas-washing plant and viewed the spot where the Peace River Bridge had so recently collapsed.

Her last stop was to see the monument built by local Fort St. John citizens to honor Alexander Mackenzie, the first white man to cross the continent.

Then it was over—a memorable day in the community's history—and Margaret's plane like a silver bird was winging into the far distance.

In the exciting forest country of big black bears and giant moose that crash through the undergrowth like steam-rollers, the princess picked out three shining gold nuggets that were panned for her by bewhiskered Alexander Moffatt and two other mud-spattered sourdoughs as they stood over their sluice box. The little scene was enacted at Prince George, British Columbia, and Margaret seemed very excited over her find. She would have something to show Charles and Anne when she got home —and the Gloucester boys as well.

St. George, with its population of fifteen hundred, lies five hundred miles northeast of Vancouver. At the airport she met another Margaret—Mrs. Margaret Seymour, who is a bright, youthful one hundred and five though she prefers to think she is two years younger.

The princess did her gold-panning in the wide Fraser

River at a spot where once Alexander Mackenzie and Simon Fraser, another explorer, exchanged goods with the Indians. Simon Fraser's descendant, nine-year-old Donna Maureen Pickle, had given her a Victorian posy at Fort St. John.

St. George is a timber metropolis; a place where you meet husky lumberjacks wearing bright checkered shirts, wide leather belts from which metal lodging wedges protrude, and high-topped caulked boots. They greeted Margaret with hell-for-leather grins and Margaret loved it. In her girlish sleeveless dress of blue and white organza she brought glamor to these rough, good-hearted men from the wilderness. She tapped her way down the dusty streets in her navy and white pumps with the smart Cuban heels while the men stood on tiptoe, some from the insides of the saloons which, unlike those at Fort St. John, were open.

Before she left St. George on the royal train which had been waiting for her she made friends with Bonnie, a twenty-six-year-old pack pony, laden with packs, axes and frying pans.

Then, standing on the observation deck like the leading lady in a Hollywood movie, Margaret waved goodby to the sourdoughs, their wives and sweethearts, as the train moved off toward the sunset.

At Williams Lake, British Columbia, Princess Margaret had a stagecoach ride she will never forget.

Now Princess Margaret knows a good horse when she sees one and she was rather skeptical of the two old plow horses from Manitoba recruited to draw her coach.

Three times during the official welcome at the railway station they reared back and almost bolted. Margaret conferred with her aides before deciding to board the coach and then she was able to stay on the seat only by hanging to a brace on either side. She got quite a shaking in the antique contraption that had no doors and was a relic of pony express days.

The horses broke into a gallop as they approached the main street and then, when finally at a standstill, tried to bolt again—and Margaret was thrown back in her seat. She stood up and tried to adjust her dress but the same thing happened again. On the third attempt she managed to climb out and drove the rest of the way by car to the rodeo grounds. It had been a rough stage debut but Margaret didn't complain.

The cowpokes of the adventurous Chicotin country, together with Indians from neighboring reservations, had arranged their own royal command performance in her honor. For days the performers had been streaming into town with their families. The familiar bouquet-presenting was a little different this time, for the lucky child, Diana Peterson, eight, had been blind all her life. At the last moment the girl burst into tears and Margaret felt like crying too. She hastily leaned forward and spoke a few reassuring words to the youngster.

For lunch the princess had flapjacks, scrambled eggs and bacon, with strong coffee to wash it down. The meal was prepared on a chuck wagon that had been drawn into the fair grounds. Margaret must have been hungry, for she pleased her host by asking for a second helping of flapjacks.

"My, how she eats," said a Shuswap Indian lady from behind her colorful blanket shawl. "Didn't they feed her in England?"

Margaret, seated in a newly whitewashed grandstand, was visibly excited at the prospect of so many ten-gallon hats and Indian braves. Witch Doctor, a contrary roan, refused to get up in his chute even for Margaret. His rider, Tom Elkins, a Shuswap Indian from Alexis Creek, looked most upset. He and Witch Doctor were to have had the honor of being first in the field.

"Let's rodeo. . . . Let's rodeo . . ." the cry went up, and then things really got started. Whooping Indians and equally noisy cowboys periodically rode, leapt into the air and were unseated. One of them got kicked in the stomach. Margaret jumped up and down almost as much as the performers. She was given a ten-gallon hat but declined to wear it; paid her respects to Princess Lorraine Squinhan, an Indian girl colorfully attired in buckskin; and had to be told four times when it was time to leave. The Margaret Rose Rodeo was over.

If she was glad of the rest and privacy that Kelowna on Lake Okanagan was to offer her, Princess Margaret didn't show it. So far she had enjoyed every minute of her Canadian trip and was eager for more. News from home was reassuring. Elizabeth's temperature was going back to normal and she was gradually recovering from her painful illness.

Summergrove Farm, an eleven-room house, was screened off from other holiday-makers by a new barbed-wire fence, a gravel wall and a formidable barrier of mounted policemen. Kelowna's population is always swelled with tourists during the summer months and Margaret's stay had attracted even more than the usual number.

A tourist camp with its crowded assortment of tents, trailers and cabins stood just beyond the six-foot-high gravel wall. The lake itself was alive with the buzz of small craft. It is a glorious spot, as blue as the Mediterranean, with a purple haze of mountains in the background.

The farm itself consists of twenty-four acres, many of them still wooded. The house is painted brown and green, and Margaret's bedroom looked out on the fairy-tale wharf. It was the perfect vacation choice for anybody. Fit for a princess who is very religious, the lovely little Church of St. Michael and All Angels was close by.

Headlines in Toronto's newspaper *The Telegram* read: A HONEYMOON PREVIEW? TOWNSEND VOWED HE'D MAKE KELOWNA TRIP.

Group Captain Townsend had spent almost a week at Kelowna during his round-the-world trip following Margaret's renunciation of any plans for marriage.

Writing in *The Telegram* Laurie McKechnie said:

> The people of this friendly, flourishing town set in the midst of one of the world's most magnificent chunks of scenery are speculating on the possibility that this may be the site of a Royal honeymoon.
>
> They think it is likely that Princess Margaret is looking over this area with special interest because, if her marriage to Peter Townsend ever takes place, they might settle down here.
>
> I talked to a man today who spent a good many

hours with Townsend, chatting, target shooting, fishing and hiking. The man, who must remain unidentified, told me that Townsend never mentioned the name of the Princess but he did say very positively: "If I married again, I should like to bring my wife here."

Johnnie Hempseed, the head bartender of the Royal Anne Hotel told me he was used to visitors exclaiming about the beauties of this area.

"But I don't think I ever talked to anyone so enthusiastic about this place as Mr. Townsend. He was really a nice, friendly chap.

"He came into my bar three or four times. He sat on that stool right there—third from the end—and he was always telling me I didn't appreciate the wonderful country I lived in. He was around here for the better part of a week.

"Of course I never heard him mention that business about the Princess. He was a real gentleman. Naturally, I didn't bring the matter up either. But two or three times he said to me, 'You know, I'd like to come and live here some day.' "

Nev Armstrong, owner of the Royal Anne, said the group captain spent most of his time with Richard Pape, a British writer who was living just outside the town then. Townsend and Pape had been together in the Royal Air Force and they were both members of the Pathfinders' Club in London.

"Mr. Townsend stayed a few days with Mr. Pape across the lake, but he used to drop in at my hotel occasionally. I offered to let him have a private lounge to have his drink in and avoid some people who seemed to be curious about him, but he preferred to sit up at the bar."

Mr. Armstrong admitted that he had heard the rumors and talk that if the group captain ever married the Princess he would bring her here.

"But he certainly never said anything like that to me. He did say repeatedly that he thought this section of the country was magnificent and he said he'd like to live here. But that was all."

Everyone in town, including Mr. Armstrong, is convinced that the long weekend on the lakeshore ten miles outside town was included in Princess Margaret's itinerary on the strength of the group captain's recommendations.

"I don't know how much truth there is in it," said Mr. Armstrong, "but everybody here is sure accepting it as true."

Margaret plainly liked what she found from the first moment of her arrival at Kelowna. The famed Okanagan Lake Monster—nearly as world-renowned as his brother at Loch Ness in Scotland—didn't lift his head out of the water. Others were there, however, to greet her, including the most eligible bachelor in the valley, Russell James Bennett, twenty-seven, son of the premier. Less than half an hour before, he had been working in his hardware store down the street.

Mayor Dick Parkinson in black robes and golden chain, Heather Watson, 1958's local "Lady of the Heather," and a host of youngsters, many of whom were still in their swimsuits, were also on hand.

Margaret found time during her vacation break to dedicate a floral clock that cost $3,500 and to open a new bridge on the lake. She also gave the officials goose-pimples by taking the notion to walk instead of ride a distance of eight hundred yards to dedicate some plaques. She didn't get jostled and no undressed Dukhobor popped up, like a purple people eater, to shock her.

Meanwhile, back in England, Canada was much in the

news. Margaret's mother accepted a twelve-ton totem pole from the government and people of British Columbia to commemorate their centenary, on behalf of the Queen.

The Queen Mother was received by Canada's High Commissioner George Drew among an avenue of Canadian trees planted to commemorate the work of the Canadian Forestry Corps during World War I.

She said that Queen Elizabeth was "very disappointed" to miss the ceremony, but was "most grateful" to British Columbia for the totem pole.

Of Princess Margaret she said, "She has been deeply touched by the wonderful welcome she has everywhere received in British Columbia."

Then the London *Daily Mail* reported that Sandra Seagram, twenty-year-old Toronto debutante, when presented at court in Buckingham Palace, gave Prince Philip "a little wink."

She was last in line at the final presentation ceremony for debutantes—the Queen having decided to do without such gatherings in future.

Kei-Deth-Be-Doo, meaning "The little Princess," was the Indian name given to Margaret during her visit to Courtenay, British Columbia. She had accepted an invitation sent her by the Native Brotherhood which includes all of British Columbia's Indians to join them in a festival of "joyous welcome."

It was a beautiful welcome, proud and sincere—one of the most stirring she received during her stay in the dominion. The Reverend Dr. Peter Kelly, a much beloved Indian, had the honor of introducing the chiefs to the newly christened Kei-Deth-Be-Doo. When eighty-eight-year-old Chief Billy Assu, who was wearing a weasel-skin war bonnet, seemed to falter on the dais steps Margaret stepped forward to help him. Once more she had shattered protocol in a gentle gesture toward the aged. However, Chief Billy, wearing his glittering medals and dried beak ornaments, managed to get up the steps without her offered assistance.

Then Chief One Big Mountain and his brother Indians gave their own interpretation of the Wild Man Dance. The dancers shuffled through their long routines, tom toms boomed, Indian maidens sang in high clear voices. Sharlene Assu, Chief Billy's ten-year-old grand-daughter, took a step backward after presenting Marga-ret with a bouquet and nearly fell off the stage!

After the performance Margaret made it her business to stop at a hospital to visit Robert Clifton, President of the Native Brotherhood, who had done much toward arranging the pageant just put on in her honor.

Afterward from his wheelchair he said, "I am the happiest and most privileged man in the world."

Lorraine McAllister, the television singer, received a lot of fan mail giving her advice as to what to sing for Princess Margaret at the Lieutenant-Governor's ball in Vancouver. One letter included twenty-five verses, some of which rhymed and some didn't.

"You know, she is the one great person who really recognizes jazz and we appreciate that," the very thrilled Lorraine said.

Lorraine's husband, orchestra leader Dal Richards, had this to say about Margaret: "We're going to amuse her by what we do normally. We feel that's as good as we can do. And if we can reach her before midnight with our music, and I think we will, I'm sure she'll stay on and have a good time. You read about her staying on later after everybody leaves the dance and taking her shoes off and really enjoying the music."

After British Columbia, Margaret journeyed on through Canada scattering good will wherever she went.

At Prince Albert, Saskatchewan, she was delighted to visit an ordinary farmer and his family. To Peder and Alvina Skotheim this came as a pleasant reward for twenty-five years of hard work on the land.

They had arrived there in 1933 with six horses and four head of cattle. The half-cleared homestead then comprised 160 acres. They dug five wells by hand but none of them was very successful. Then they called in the services of a professional well-digger and in 1936 "the well came in." The Skotheim's house has a new refrigerator and a propane gas stove in the large combination kitchen-dining room. They have a piano and television for amusement. Drinking water is carried in from the precious well.

"I was speechless when our member of Parliament, Mr. McIntosh, told me we were chosen for the visit," said Mrs. Skotheim. "She's royalty and we're ordinary people, so I didn't know what to do. I almost refused. But I felt better after we'd talked to her aide. He said to talk to her like anybody else, and made us believe she's just like us, or almost like us." And Mrs. Skotheim did!

Margaret landed by helicopter in the pasture behind the red barn where the black and white Holsteins usually graze. They had been temporarily moved to the corrals beforehand.

She visited the piggery and walked through the cotton-weed trees into the garden where she admired the peonies and sweet-smelling honeysuckle, so reminiscent of an ordinary English cottage garden. She saw the little log cabin the original homesteader built in 1908 that was Peder and Alvina's first home on their land.

Peder, the son of Siverts Skotheim of Modle, Romsdalen Province, Norway, started out in life as a fisherman, as generations of his family had done before him. He didn't like fishing and in his own words: "I came to Canada in 1923 and worked as a hired man near Saskatoon for fifty dollars a month. When I had a thousand dollars saved in 1928, I started out on my own with six horses and some machinery, mostly on credit. I rented land." Then in 1933 he bought his own farm and married the district schoolteacher, Alvina Hansen, who was of Norwegian descent.

They put in no crops the first year but cut hay and hauled logs in from the bush. Now they own six hundred acres of Saskatchewan farm land having a hundred acres each in oats, barley, and wheat and the rest in tame hay and pasture.

There are ten Skotheim children.

Just outside Ottawa the princess copied a lot of other Canadians and spent some time at the "summer cottage." It wasn't most people's idea of a cottage, though, for this one had princely proportions—ten bedrooms and five bathrooms. It was the summer home of Prime Minister and Mrs. John Diefenbaker at Harrington Lake.

Once more Margaret took to a helicopter, landing on the lawn among the petunia beds. She had the place to herself for two days, the narrow road and green hills encircling the lake being well guarded against the curious. Mrs. Diefenbaker left Margaret the large megaphone with which she always calls her husband in from his fishing on the lake.

The "cottage," which Margaret loved, had new curtains and slipcovers in cream, brown, gold and green for the royal visit. It is cedar-paneled inside and the windows of the larger rooms let in plenty of sunshine. A huge rough-stone fireplace is the main feature of the twenty-six-foot living room, and here the princess learned to pop corn and toast marshmallows.

The princess had a bedroom above the living room with a beautiful view from the windows on three sides. A bedroom suite was moved from the prime minister's town house for her use.

A hemp-rope ladder as a fire precaution hung down from one of the windows, and a bold sign, NO SMOKING ON THIS FLOOR, was plainly displayed for Margaret to see. Whether she observed it was anybody's guess, for she had certainly replaced the long cigarette holder she dropped from a train in a forested section of British Columbia.

At the Stratford Shakespearean Festival she turned up to see *The Winter's Tale,* for which Tanya Moiseiwitsch had found inspirations for the stage settings in Rubens paintings. The flavor of the Seventeenth-Century costumes delighted the fashion-interested princess who is equally keen on all aspects of stage costumes and production.

In Montreal she attended a performance staged by La Comédie Canadienne and, at Calgary, a miniature re-enactment of the famed cowboy stampede. At Toronto she made a royal progress as exciting as any that the great lover of progresses, Queen Elizabeth I, ever made.

In Quebec City Margaret found all the old-world charm of New France. She toured the Plains of Abraham where two equally gentlemanly soldiers, Wolfe and Montcalm, decided Canada's destiny in 1759, and was affectionately received by the citizens.

The brief visit recalled the days of Frontenac's merry court and when Margaret left the good people of Quebec she took with her their motto which carried all the sentiments of her first wonderful visit to Canada—*JE ME SOUVIENS—I remember.*

Chapter Twenty-eight

THE FUTURE

What does the future hold for Princess Margaret? Will she ever marry? Will she be appointed a governor-general in one of her sister's far-flung dominions? These are questions we hear from time to time.

One thing is certain. Suggestions may be made but nobody will ever tell Princess Margaret what she must do.

At the time the Townsend crisis came to a head she had consulted no one. Even her own mother and sister had no idea of what she intended to do. A court official speaking of that unhappy period has said, "Until the last minute everybody at the palace was in an absolute frenzy preparing to deal with the constitutional issues involved if she decided to marry him."

If she does receive a governor-general's post she will make a great success of the job, for she has always wanted to be a personality in her own right. She has never wanted to overshadow the Queen; she is still passionately fond of her sister.

She is exceptionally interested in women's rights and attended a debate in the stately House of Lords calling for the admission of women as life peers to that traditional institution.

Friends intimate that if she ever does marry the bridegroom's qualifications must be as follows:

British or at least brought up in Britain.

A practising Christian and a regular churchgoer.

A man who has a regular job whether he is in need of the money or not.

A man who likes the sophisticated life of the city as well as the joys of the countryside.

Must be a good mixer and not a snob.

Must have an interest in the arts.

One thing he need not be—and that is of royal blood.

Eric Nicol, writing in the Winnipeg *Tribune*, once said: "It is my impression that, if she were free to do as she pleased, Princess Margaret would have sought an adventurous career in films or become an airline stewardess, or else married some hairy fellow whose answer to most domestic problems was a slap on the backside." Many other observers think the same.

Back in 1944 Princess Margaret, then still a schoolgirl, wrote a letter to qualify for her hostess badge in the Girl Guides.

The sad little make-believe letter might easily have

been written by the proverbial fairy tale princess, for it ended: "I shall do my very best to bring a partner, and would Lord Tulip do?"

Princess Margaret is still searching for Lord Tulip.

1947.   South African Tour taken with parents and sister.

1948.   Special mission to the Netherlands for enthronement of Queen Juliana.

1949.   Grand tour of Italy, Switzerland and France.

1950.   Visit to Malta with sister.

1951.   Second visit to France.

1953.   Visit to Norway for wedding of Princess Ragnhild.

1953.   Tour of Rhodesia undertaken with the Queen Mother.

1954.   Visit to Western Germany.

1955.   First tour of the Caribbean.

1956.   Visit to Sweden to join sister and brother-in-law.

1956.   Tour of East Africa.

1958.   Second visit to Western Germany.
Second tour of the Caribbean and first visit to British Guiana.
First tour of Canada.